THREE APPROACHES TO CLASSROOM MANAGEMENT

Views from a Psychological Perspective

Jerry D. Lehman

UNIVERSITY
PRESS OF
AMERICA

Copyright © 1982 by
University Press of America, Inc.
P.O. Box 19101, Washington, D.C. 20036

Library of Congress Cataloging in Publication Data

Lehman, Jerry D.
   Three approaches to classroom management.

   Includes bibliographical references.
   1. Classroom management. 2. School discipline.
I. Title.
LB3011.L35 1982   371.1'024   81-43843
ISBN 0-8191-2572-5
ISBN 0-8191-2573-3 (pbk.)

Dedicated to my wife

Faye

and to our children

Lynn and Leigh

THREE APPROACHES TO CLASSROOM MANAGEMENT

TABLE OF CONTENTS

PREFACE

This book presents three approaches to managing students' behavior in elementary and secondary school classrooms. Many teachers and administrators perceive discipline as the most pressing problem facing the schools. Even though the problem is apparent, frequently teachers feel that they are unprepared to deal with the disruptive behavior which confronts them each day. Therefore, this book is directed to teachers and prospective teachers who are seeking new ideas concerning how to deal with students. The approach I have taken is unique for a book of this type. I examine the ideas of psychologists who come from three different orientations (behavioral, reality, and humanistic) and then look at the application of each orientation to classroom management. Thus, the book is grounded in theory and also contains pertinent material concerning how these theoretical concepts can be put to use in the classroom. It is my hope that teachers and students will find this book helpful as an introduction to classroom management and as a guide to implementing various management procedures.

CHAPTER 1

CLASSROOM MANAGEMENT: AN INTRODUCTION

"I have just about had it with that class. Yesterday it was one problem after another and today was no different. It's been that way all semester. I've already sent four students to the principal's office this week. About half the students are unmanageable and the few who want to learn can't because of all the distractions. I go home with a headache every day. To tell the truth, I just don't know what I'm going to do."

Experiences like this are common in almost every school. Some teachers learn to cope. Others leave the teaching profession because of their inability to manage students' behavior. In a recent Phi Delta Kappan poll (September 1977), educators rated discipline as their number one concern. Studies (Stephens and Evans, 1973) show that beginning teachers are especially worried. As many as 70 percent express fears about their ability to control students' behavior. Members of the community also perceive the problem. When parents were asked in a Gallup poll (Smith and Gallup, 1977), "What do you think are the biggest problems with which the public schools in this comunity must deal?" they rated lack of discipline as the number one problem facing the schools.

How Real Is the Problem?

There are reasons for teachers to be alarmed. A report by the Department of Health, Education, and Welfare (1972) indicated that of every five children, one will exhibit excessive or problem behavior. The work of other researchers seems to support this finding (e.g., Swift, Spivack, Danset, Danset-Leger and Winnykamen, 1972).

It would also appear that vandalism of school property and violence toward teachers are on the increase. The Wall Street Journal on February 3, 1976, reported that during the 1974-75 school year, students were involved in 270,000 school burglaries and acts of vandalism resulting in $600 million in property damage. The Senate Subcommittee on Juvenile Delinquency in 1975 reported that between 1970 and 1973 there was a 77 percent increase in student assaults on teachers. Findings like these indicate that students are becoming

1

more unmanageable and emphasize the need for more effective control within the school and classroom environment. If research statistics seem far removed from the real world, a discussion with a group of teachers or a school visit may bring the problem closer to home. Certainly, any teacher can attest that there is no shortage of behavioral problems in the public schools.

Who Is Responsible?

It is easy to point an accusing finger at someone else when assessing responsibility. "It's the teacher's fault" or "the administration is too lax," or "there's no discipline in the home." Regardless of the cause of the problem, the fact remains: the teacher is responsible for managing the behavior of students in the classroom.

So Bobby Is a Discipline Problem

Mrs. Brown noticed Bobby the very first day. He was constantly seeking attention in negative ways. If he wasn't fighting he was finding other ways to keep the class in an uproar. After two weeks of his disruptions, Mrs. Brown could stand it no longer. A frantic call to the school psychologist resulted in several days of testing. At least Bobby was out of the room during this time and maybe the results would indicate why Bobby was such a problem. After a series of tests and a conference with Bobby's mother, the psychologist reported his findings. Bobby comes from a broken home. He lives with his mother who must work the second shift, so Bobby is left to roam the streets after school. He is very hostile due to his broken home, harsh treatment and lack of love. The tests all indicate that Bobby perceives the world in a negative way. "Yes," the psychologist reports, "all indications are that Bobby will be a problem student."

There are many Bobby's in the school system. After attempting to deal with their constant disruptions, we get angry and frustrated. After learning about their backgrounds, we may feel pity and sadness. We are tempted to blame the parents and to give up in our effort to help them since we are constantly reminded of the fact that we cannot change their home life. But Bobby is still there. He is still a student in the class and his behavior is still disruptive.

2

Students like Bobby are not easy to handle. It takes time, patience, and knowledge of effective management skills to produce positive results. Understanding a child's background may be informative but rarely can the child's home situation be changed; therefore, teachers must focus their efforts on helping students learn to behave appropriately in the classroom. This is a major responsibility and can determine the teacher's success or failure. Dr. Hiam Ginott, author of Teacher and Child, summed it up in this way:

> I have come to a frightening conclusion. I am the decisive element in the classroom. It is my personal approach that creates the climate. It is my daily mood that makes the weather. As a teacher I possess tremendous power to make a child's life miserable or joyous. I can be a tool of torture or an instrument of inspiration. I can humiliate or humor, hurt or heal. In all situations it is my response that decides whether a crisis will be escalated or de-escalated, and a child humanized or de-humanized (1972, p. 15).

What Is Classroom Management?

The term classroom management has many different connotations. Perhaps the most familiar is represented by the idea that the effectively managed classroom is one where the students are quiet, orderly, and polite. This view interprets any disruption as undesirable and a threat to effective control. Such a viewpoint appears to be restrictive and for this reason it is suggested that a broader, more positive approach be taken. Long and Frye (1977) take such an approach when they state that "classroom management includes all that teachers do to help students acquire useful skills and the purpose is always to facilitate teaching--not merely to control or keep order." Classroom management viewed in this light includes more than the elimination of undesirable behavior; it also involves the learning of desirable behavior. Management problems occur when students engage in behaviors which interfere with the progress of both social and academic learning. The task of teachers is to help students learn appropriate responses while inhibiting inappropriate ones. The challenge for teachers is evident. They must ask how they can best help students learn both social and academic skills. With this attitude teachers are less likely to see students as problems and more likely to perceive them as needing help in learning new skills.

3

Approaches to Classroom Management

There is no scarcity of suggestions concerning what administrators and teachers should do to improve the schools. Cases have been made for more discipline, less discipline, smaller classes, more teachers, and a better curriculum. Theories to explain why students misbehave are also prevalent. It has been argued that children need more love, they are bored, they are seeking attention, they are hyperactive, they don't trust adults and they just can't read well. While all the discussion continues, problems increase at an alarming rate.

In the midst of the discussion, teachers are left to face the day-to-day problems of classroom management. They look to educators and administrators but frequently come away with ideas which are of little help in implementing workable solutions. They look to school psychologists but too often are given only test results explaining why students misbehave. Teachers need workable solutions which are action oriented and point the way to improving management skills. Although no suggested solutions are going to solve all the teachers' problems, the situation is certainly not hopeless. Teachers who are willing to admit their problems and search for new answers have a good chance of becoming more effective. Strategies do exist which can be useful in helping teachers cope with management difficulties and the frustrations of teaching. These strategies may not always be easy to implement (trying new approaches usually takes courage) but they offer some valuable help. The purpose of this book is to present three approaches for dealing with classroom management problems. Each of these approaches stresses action and specifies what teachers can do to more effectively manage students' behavior and promote learning. Each approach has been successfully implemented in the classroom and encompasses ideas, techniques, and management procedures which have potential usefulness for every teacher. Although each teacher must find his or her own approach to teaching, understanding the ideas and suggestions of others can broaden the teacher's options. An understanding of these three approaches should allow teachers to choose those aspects of an approach which best fit their teaching style.

What Lies Ahead

Each of the following three chapters presents an approach to classroom management. In each chapter there is a discussion of the ideas, experiences, or research studies which led to the development of the approach. Attention is then given to how the concepts of the approach apply to schools and the management of students' behavior. The case examples at the end of each chapter provide research evidence for the effectiveness of each approach. Involvement exercises are presented for each chapter and are perceived to be an important aspect of the book. Too often reading involves a quick scanning of material without eliciting the reader's response. The exercises are provided to help teachers and prospective teachers understand the approaches, crystallize their thinking, and explore their feelings. Reader responses will enhance recall of the material and provide an opportunity to practice aspects of the approach in hypothetical situations. Hopefully in assimilating the material and responding to the exercises the teacher can use what has been learned to more effectively manage behavior.

REFERENCES

Ginott, H. _Teacher and Child_. New York: The Macmillan Company, 1972.

Long, J. D., and Frye, H. F. _Making it till Friday_. Princeton, N.J.: Princeton Book Company, 1977.

"Our nation's schools--a report card: 'A' in school violence and vandalism." United States Subcommittee Report on Juvenile Delinquency. Washington, D.C.: U.S. Government Printing Office, 1975.

Smith, V., and Gallup, G. H. _What the people think about their schools: Gallup's findings_. Bloomington, Indiana: Phi Delta Kappa Educational Foundation, 1977.

Stephens, J. M., and Evans, E. D. _Development and classroom learning: An introduction to educational psychology_. New York: Holt, Rinehart and Winston, 1973.

Swift, M. S., Spivack, G., Danset, A., Danset-Leger, J., and Winnykomen, F. "Classroom behavior and academic success of French and American elementary school children." _International Review of Applied Psychology_, 1972, 20, 1-11.

United States Department of Health, Education, and Welfare, Public Health Services. "Behavior patterns of children in schools." Vital health statistics 11, 1972, 1-78.

CHAPTER 2

THE BEHAVIORAL APPROACH TO CLASSROOM MANAGEMENT

It is impossible to understand the behavioral approach to classroom management without first understanding the concepts of both classical and operant conditioning. John Watson, who founded the school of thought known as behaviorism, accepted the principles of learning set forth by Ivan Pavlov. Pavlov, working with dogs in his laboratory, came to realize that an animal can learn (be conditioned) to salivate to a sound such as a buzzer if the buzzer is paired with a stimulus which automatically produces salivation. The conditioning procedure works in the following way:

1. The neutral or conditioned stimulus, in this case the buzzer, is first presented.

2. The stimulus, food, immediately follows the buzzer. This stimulus is referred to as the unconditioned stimulus since the animal automatically salivates to the food. Salivation in this instance is said to be a biologically innate response.

3. The salivation response to the food is referred to as the unconditioned response. Salivation to the food is automatic. It does not have to be learned.

4. After numerous pairings between the conditioned stimulus (buzzer) and the unconditioned stimulus (food), the conditioned stimulus comes to elicit the same response as the unconditioned stimulus. Therefore, salivation to the buzzer alone is the conditioned or learned response. This whole procedure is known as classical or respondent conditioning.

Since Pavlov's classic study with dogs, other researchers have verified this form of learning in other animals and humans. Pavlov's ideas were popularized in America by John Watson, who is referred to as the father of behaviorism.

The Work of John Watson

In 1920 John Watson published one of the most famous conditioning experiments in the annals of

7

psychology. Watson believed that humans, too, learned responses through the process of association described by Pavlov. To test this hypothesis, Watson selected an eleven-month-old child named Albert to be a subject in his conditioning experiment. Albert was a very unemotional lad who exhibited no signs of fear to a rat, a rabbit, a monkey, a dog, or a burning newspaper. The one event which seemed to elicit a fear response in Albert was a loud noise produced by striking a steel bar with a hammer. Conditioning began when Watson placed a white rat near Albert. When the boy reached for the rat, the loud noise was sounded. Albert, of course, was startled. Upon recovery from the initial shock, he again reached for the rat and again the noise caused him to jump and this time to whimper. In order not to seriously disturb the child Watson decided to wait a few days to condinue conditioning. One week later, after five more conditioning trials, Albert was noticeably affected by the rat's presence. The previously unemotional child now cried loudly and attempted to escape. Watson believed that this provided evidence that an emotional response to a specific object or situation could be the product of a simple form of learning. This learning involved pairing a neutral stimulus (rat) with an unconditioned stimulus (loud noise) until the neutral stimulus (rat) produced the same response (fear--crying and escape) as the loud noise automatically produced.

Classical Conditioning: What's in It for the Teacher

A journey back into the world of Pavlov and Watson may seem irrelevant to the teacher who is interested in learning how to manage students' behavior. Pavlov's and Watson's works are important because they provided the groundwork for a better understanding of behavior in a variety of settings including the school. Although teachers are not interested in reflex responses like salivation, they are usually concerned about attitudes and emotional responses exhibited by their students. This is true partly because attitudes and emotions are reflected in behavior. It may even be best to think of attitudes/emotions and behavior occurring together. Watson not only referred to Albert's fear, but he also described behaviors such as crying and attempting to escape which provided the basis for inferring fear. How do we know that Johnny has a negative attitude toward math or a positive attitude toward recess? We can only know this by observing Johnny's behavior. If Johnny says "I can't wait till recess" and runs toward the door when the bell rings, his visible behavior would indicate an approach tendency in regard to recess. Robert Mager (1968) has pointed out that those things for which we have approach tendencies are usually things for which we have a positive feeling or attitude. Conversely, those things for which we tend to avoid or move away from are frequently those things for which we have a negative feeling or attitude. Therefore, knowledge of classical conditioning can help teachers understand how children learn positive and negative attitudes. With this understanding, perhaps teachers can help children develop positive attitudes and approach tendencies toward school stimuli.

Classical Conditioning: An Example

Suppose you are a piano teacher and one of your goals is to help students develop positive attitudes toward playing the piano. Sammy, one of your new students, is ten years old and has looked forward to taking piano lessons for several years. She shows up the first day very excited, but nervous about her new learning experience. What is the next step? What can you do to continue to help her develop approach tendencies? What might happen which would make her want to avoid the situation? We cannot be entirely sure how this example will turn out. There are many variables which will influence the outcome, such as Sammy's ability, the amount of reinforcement from parents and friends and, of course, the behavior of the teacher. The teacher's behavior is probably the only means the teacher has of shaping the outcome. Is it enough? Here again we cannot be certain; however, it is important to remember that the attitudes or tendencies students develop toward an object or activity will be determined by what is associated with that object or activity. It is the teacher's responsibility to provide the things which help students develop positive attitudes and approach tendencies toward learning rather than negative attitudes and avoidance tendencies.

Classical Conditioning: A Reassessment

If we look at the examples used so far we can see the influence of conditioning.

Pavlov's Dogs

Buzzer sounded ———→ followed by ———→ salivation
food   to food

Buzzer sounded ——————————→ salivation to buzzer

Conditioning has occurred when the dog salivates to the buzzer.

Little Albert

Rat presented ———→ followed by ———→ fear--crying
loud noise   and escape

Rat presented ——————————→ fear--crying and escape

Conditioning has occurred when Albert cries and attempts to escape from the rat.

Sammy's piano lesson

The piano, the ——→ possibly followed by ——→ tendencies to
teacher and the   praise, punishment,   either ap-
piano lesson   advice, ridicule,   proach or
                    frustration, anxiety,   avoid, to
                    success, failure, etc.   feel positive
                                               or negative

The piano, the ——————————→ tendencies to approach or
teacher and the   avoid, to feel positive
piano lesson   or negative

Conditioning has occurred when the student develops either approach or avoidance tendencies toward the teacher and piano instruction.

Let us carry this example format one step further and project ourselves into a school situation.

The student at school

The teacher, ——→ followed by those ——→ tendencies to
the school, the   things over which   approach or
subject matter,   the teacher has some   avoid, to feel
etc.   control and which   positive or
                    help students to   negative
                    develop either ap-
                    proach or avoidance
                    tendencies

10

The teacher, the ————————▶ tendencies to approach or
school, the sub-   avoid, to feel positive or
ject matter, etc.   negative

Conditioning has occurred when the student develops approach or avoidance tendencies toward the subject
matter, the teacher, or perhaps even the school.

Positive and negative attitudes are often reflected in student comments. "I can't wait to go to
4th period" or "I hate going to math, let's cut today"
are responses which reflect approach and avoidance
tendencies. Remember, the teacher does not control all
the variables which determine what attitudes and response tendencies develop toward learning. But if
teachers are to have an influence they must be mindful
of the fact that it is the things which happen to the
student while in the presence of school stimuli which
determine what attitudes and response tendencies
develop.

Encouraging Negative Attitudes
and Avoidance Tendencies

Very few teachers consciously set out to encourage
negative attitudes toward learning. When this does
happen it is usually an unintentional by-product of the
teacher's attempt to manage the classroom. Ask yourself what situations individuals avoid. Is it not
those situaitons which have been found to be aversive?
Of course what is aversive for one individual may not
be for another, but there are some things which most
everyone finds distasteful.

Individuals usually avoid people or situations
which are associated with physical pain or discomfort.
Some teachers still resort to the use of physical punishment as a method of managing students' behavior.
If this punishment is administered by the teacher or a
school authority, there is always the possibility of
increasing negative attitudes and avoidance tendencies
toward those things associated with the pain--the
teacher, the school, the subject matter. Put another
way, students may develop attitudes and feelings which
interfere with tendencies to learn. A principle recently commented that it is those students who already
have a negative attitude toward school who are most
likely the recipients of physical punishment; thus,
further alienating them from any chance of developing
a positive attitude.

Individuals usually also prefer to avoid people or situations which are associated with psychological distress or discomfort. Students and teachers dislike being humiliated, embarrassed, frustrated, threatened, fussed at and labeled failures. Yet sometimes in an attempt to manage behavior, teachers believe they must use such measures. Regardless of how necessary these practices are, this does not alter their effect. When these conditions are associated with school stimuli, then the teacher, the subject matter or the school may be viewed in a less favorable light.

Practices which are likely to be associated with the development of negative attitudes and avoidance tendencies include the following:

* Verbally berating students in front of their peers for poor performance.

* Asking students to perform tasks and solve problems which are far beyond their level of ability.

* Repeatedly communicating to students that they are failures.

* Testing over material which has not been assigned.

* Failure to listen to the students' point of view and to take their feelings into consideration.

* Presenting information in a boring, uninteresting manner.

* Threatening students with all kinds of harsh consequences if behavior or performance does not improve.

* Administering harsh physical punishment when students violate rules.

Encouraging Positive Attitudes and Approach Tendencies

A goal of education is to help students develop a positive attitude toward learning. Rather than associate schools with physical and psychological discomfort, ways must be found to associate the learning situation with pleasant events and consequences. Many teachers are very good at creating conditions which

12

help students feel good about themselves, the subject matter, and the school. These teachers actively seek ways to associate classroom activities with positive, pleasant experiences.

Practices which are likely to be associated with the development of positive attitudes and approach tendencies include the following:

* Making students feel that they are important and that the teacher is concerned about them regardless of their behavior.

* Listening to the students' point of view and accepting their feelings.

* Reinforcing and recognizing a student's accomplishments regardless of how small they might be.

* Communicating clearly to students what is expected of them.

* Providing interesting ways of presenting material such as varying the method of presentation, getting students actively involved, and relating subject matter to relevant experience.

* Allowing students to work on material which is appropriate for their learning level.

* Allowing students to help develop classroom rules so that they feel somewhat personally responsible for the learning environment.

* Emphasizing the good qualities that students possess rather than focusing on negatives.

Remember, (1) positive or negative attitudes and emotions can be conditioned to school stimuli. (2) The attitudes students develop may depend on the behavior of the teacher. (3) Students' attitudes are usually reflected in their behavior. (4) Students with positive attitudes are more cooperative and usually want to approach learning activities. (5) Students with negative attitudes are more difficult to manage and frequently avoid learning activities.

Operant Conditioning

While Pavlov and Watson stressed behavior which was elicited by a known stimulus such as salivation to food and then salivation to a buzzer, B. F. Skinner, another behaviorist, emphasized behavior which is not linked to any known stimulus. Although Skinner believes that behavior is caused by stimulation, in most instances the source of the stimulation is unknown. As an individual behaves or operates in an environment, it is not a preceding stimulus which is important but rather what happens after the behavior occurs. Operant behavior is said to be controlled by its consequences-- by what happens after a response has been emitted. This is a different approach to learning than that offered by the classical conditioning theorists. Classical conditioning best explains one type of learning, i.e., reflex and emotional responses, whereas operant conditioning best explains another type of learning. Thus, the two views are complementary rather than contradictory. We will now turn our attention to learning principles based on operant conditioning. Then we will explore how these principles can be utilized by the teacher.

A Rat, a Box, and a Reward

B. F. Skinner is an experimental psychologist who used animals in his attempt to understand learning. He invented a small chamber, referred to as a Skinner box, for housing the rats and pigeons used in his studies. This chamber contains a lever at one end, a light, and a small food tray. The chamber can be activated so that when the lever is pressed a food pellet automatically drops into the tray. A rat placed in this box engages in exploratory behavior and at times this random responding brings the animal in contact with the lever. If the box is not activated, no food is presented and the rat continues to engage in exploratory activity. In order to condition an animal, the chamber can be activated so that any lever press is followed by a food pellet dropping into the tray. This is accompanied by a clicking noise which is produced by the apparatus when the food is delivered. As the animal explores the box a random lever press is followed by the delivery of the food reward. Since the food is easily obtainable it is soon discovered and devoured. Under these circumstances lever pressing becomes much more frequent until, of course, the animal is satiated. Having an animal trained in this way now allows other responses to be conditioned. Going to the middle of the box can be conditioned by waiting until the animal's random movements take it to the middle and then delivering the food pellet. This is accompanied by the clicking noise of the apparatus, which now serves to cue the animal that food is available. If the sound occurs while the animal is in the middle of the box, the frequency of going to the middle increases because it is reinforced by the food reward. Studies indicate that rewarding an animal for every correct response at the beginning of the procedure aids in establishing the response. After the response has been learned, intermittent or partial reinforcement is all that is needed, and even increases the likelihood that the response will continue to be emitted long after the reward is no longer given.

Even more complex responses are conditionable. Let us say we want a pigeon to make a 360 degree turn in the middle of the box, something which the animal may not do at random. First, the pigeon is rewarded for going to the middle of the box. When the animal returns to the middle, a slight turning movement is required before providing reward. The click again signals that food is available and the pigeon immediately responds. Then back to the middle of the box, except this time the animal is required to make an even greater turn before the reward is provided—and so it goes until by gradually increasing the amount of the complete response before the reward is given, the animal's behavior is shaped into a full 360 degree revolution. Conditioning a pigeon to make any one of these responses is a rather simple procedure. Decreasing the frequency of these learned responses is also relatively easy. To do so, the food reinforcer is no longer presented when the response is emitted. The response is performed less and less frequently, eventually becoming extinct.

Defining Terms

* Operant conditioning is defined as the modification of a response by following the response with consequences which either strengthen or weaken the response.

* Positive reinforcement involves adding something positive, pleasant or rewarding to the environment after a response has been made. This, of course, tends to increase the frequency of the response.

* Shaping is the gradual development of a response by reinforcing greater and greater approximations of the total response.

* Extinction occurs when an operant response is weakened by removing the reinforcer which previously followed the response.

* Continuous reinforcement involves reinforcing a response every time it occurs.

* Partial reinforcement involves reinforcing a response, not after every occurrence, but rather on an intermittent schedule. Partial reinforcement tends to increase resistance to extinction.

Back to the Rat One More Time

The preceding discussion indicated how positive reinforcement can increase the frequency of a response. Is it possible to get an animal to press the lever without adding something positive after the lever is pressed? This is possible, but it involves an aversive stimulus. For example, if the rat is placed in the Skinner box and the floor is electrified with a small current, the animal will move about rapidly. Quite by chance the animal will trip the lever and now instead of food being presented the current is turned off. The likelihood of the lever being pressed again when the floor is electrified will increase. But this time it is accomplished not by adding something positive to the environment but by removing an aversive stimulus. Increasing behavior in this way is referred to as negative reinforcement. You may recall that those things associated with aversive stimuli will be avoided. Operant conditioning principles indicate that whatever response terminates an aversive stimulus will be strengthened. If the classroom environment becomes an aversive stimulus, then those responses which terminate the aversiveness (e.g., tardiness, daydreaming, cutting class, misbehavior), will tend to be strengthened.

More Definitions

* Negative reinforcement increases the frequency of a response by following the response with the removal of something aversive from the environment.

* Reinforcement can be of two types, either positive or negative. Regardless of the type, when a response is reinforced it increases in frequency.

* Punishment, which has not yet been mentioned in relation to operant conditioning, is sometimes confused with negative reinforcement. Behaviorists define punishment in two ways. Type I punishment occurs when something aversive is added to the environment after a response has been emitted. Usually punishment is administered in order to weaken a response. Shocking a rat after a lever pressing response or spanking a child after breaking a window are examples of Type I punishment.

* Type II punishment involves removing something pleasant from the environment after a response has been made. Taking away privileges from a child after inappropriate behavior is an example of Type II punishment.

Behaviorists are cautious when discussing the advantages of punishment. Many believe that harsh forms of Type I punishment have serious drawbacks, e.g., they lead to undesirable side effects, they do not necessarily weaken a response, and their results are too unpredictable. Behaviorists are more inclined to advocate various forms of Type II punishment and feel that if used properly, in combination with positive reinforcement, these can effectively alter behavior. We will return to this subject as it applies to the classroom in a later section of this chapter.

I Teach Kids, Not Pigeons

I hope this talk about rats and pigeons has not turned you off. Most teachers would be quite content never to have a rat or pigeon inhabit their classroom. You may be wondering if anything from this work is at all relevant to teaching. Behaviorists have gathered a great deal of information which indicates that the principles of operant conditioning can be very effective in classroom situations. In recent years, the classroom application of these principles has been widespread and very helpful to many teachers. On the other hand, some teachers after reading about reinforcement and other operant procedures, have used these tools incorrectly, haphazardly, or without consideration of basic management procedures. Soon these teachers cast aside the ideas which seemed so promising because they are thought not to work. The remainder of this chapter will focus on the use of operant principles for effective classroom management.

Setting the Stage for
Effective Management

If operant conditioning principles are to be used effectively, certain conditions must be established in the classroom. These conditions set the stage for effective management and are so important they must be mentioned before proceeding further.

<u>Minimizing Undesirable Conditions</u>. Recently I visited an elementary school to talk with teachers about classroom management. We discussed many problems, but their major concern was how to control students during what was referred to as "bus room." One week a month each teacher had to supervise bus students who arrived early and stayed late. I soon was to learn that each teacher was having to supervise about fifty students in a room built to accommodate thirty-five. There were not enough desks for everyone and students were literally standing around the room or sitting on top of each other. As you can imagine, the place was chaos. The teachers were looking for suggestions which would help them maintain order and their sanity in this situation. My first response was, "There is no way to walk barefoot through the mud without getting dirty." I was trying to imply the importance of minimizing undesirable conditions before expecting any approach to be successful. This led to a brainstorming session concerning how to change bus room to minimize conditions for inappropriate behavior. As a result of this discussion, some changes were initiated which made bus room more tolerable and improved the chances of success for those teachers who did introduce new management techniques.

This example may be atypical, but in every classroom there are ways teachers can minimize conditions which interfere with learning. This may involve nothing more than moving a student from one seat to another, changing the arrangement of desks, or presenting certain material in the morning when students are alert rather than right after lunch. Whatever the situation, teachers need to identify the conditions which tend to increase appropriate behavior and then institute the needed changes. Minimizing undesirable conditions will increase the teacher's chances of success when management techniques are implemented.

<u>Establishing Classroom Rules</u>. The establishment of classroom rules alerts the student to what is appropriate and inappropriate behavior. Most

18

successful teachers realize that rules must be well
defined so that students will know what is expected of
them. Many authorities suggest that students be allowed to take part in formulating the rules. Such a suggestion seems wise for several reasons: it shows
confidence in the students' ability to cooperate by
setting reasonable rules, and it increases the likelihood that students will adhere to the rules since they
helped formulate them. Madsen and Madsen (1974, p. 181)
have provided some excellent suggestions for establishing classroom rules.

1. Involve the class in making up the rules.

2. Keep the rules short and to the point.

3. Phrase rules, when possible, in a positive
   way. ("Sit quietly while working" instead of
   "Don't talk to your neighbors.")

4. Remind the class of the rules at times other
   than when someone has misbehaved.

5. Make different sets of rules for various
   activities.

6. Let children know when different rules apply
   (work-play).

7. Post rules in a conspicuous place and review
   regularly.

8. Keep a sheet on your desk and review the
   number of times you review rules with class.

Writing rules can be difficult. Good rules need
to be clear and specific so that students know what
behaviors are acceptable and which are unacceptable.
If possible, rules should be written so that you and
your students know when a rule has been broken.

Although rules are essential, do not be led to
believe that having rules prevents all behavioral problems. As you might predict, the behaviorists believe
that it is what happens to the student after violating
or complying with the rules which determines if behavior will be strengthened or weakened.

Determining Consequences. Let us suppose that you
have established a few short rules. They are posted on
the bulletin board where they can clearly be seen.

Perhaps one of the rules states that students are to work quietly while doing seat work. Your 6th graders have worked quietly at their desks for some time on math problems until Terry begins kicking Phillip, the student sitting next to him. This distracts Phillip and he begins to kick back. What has happened? How does the teacher respond? What about the rules? When asking college students about a similar incident recently, almost everyone concentrated on the misbehavior. Inappropriate behavior stands out, perhaps because it is disruptive. The appropriate behavior of the 6th graders seemed to be ignored in the college students' discussion, even though the 6th graders engaged in more appropriate than inappropriate behavior. The point should be clear. Students engage in many types of appropriate behavior. They come to class on time, prepare their homework, work on assignments, answer questions, and comply with the rules. Teachers must not forget to provide consequences for appropriate responses. Since this is such an important point, the following discussion will first concentrate on consequences for appropriate behavior. Then we will turn our attention to inappropriate behavior.

Providing Consequences for Appropriate Behavior

By now you are familiar with the term positive reinforcement. A positive reinforcer is a stimulus or event that strengthens the behavior which it follows. There are, of course, many stimuli and events which can serve as positive reinforcers. Some examples are food, money, attention, and praise. In this discussion we are interested in positive reinforcers which can be used as consequences for strengthening appropriate behavior in the classroom. There are several potentially powerful reinforcers which deserve attention here.

Praise. Most students enjoy a pat on the back or a word of praise for a job well done. Sometimes we forget about and even underestimate the importance of praise. If praise can be offered sincerely and naturally it can make the student feel good about himself as well as strengthen behaviors which it follows. Young children, especially, enjoy knowing that what they have done is appreciated. Some individuals have trouble praising people for what they feel should naturally be expected of them. This has been such a problem in business organizations that managers have attended workshops where role-playing has been used to help them learn to reinforce more effectively with praise.

erhaps many teachers could benefit from using praise
more often. However, do not expect all students to
respond immediately to your praise. Some children have
grown up in homes where praise has not been associated
with things which are naturally reinforcing, such as
food and attention. Because of this they have not
learned to value praise. With these students the
teacher may need to make a special effort to associate
praise with a known reinforcer so that the praise and
approval of the teacher become valued. For example,
telling a student who has successfully completed a task
that because of his good work he can help with the film
strip projector may be helpful. Again, don't expect
praise to immediately become reinforcing but remember
the continued pairing of positive attention and a known
reinforcer may eventually make the teacher's praise and
approval a valued reinforcer.

Attention. As you realize, praise and approval
are forms of positive attention and can be used to
strengthen behavior. As contradictory as it may seem,
the opposite of positive attention, negative attention
such as scoldings and reprimands may also strengthen
the behaviors which they follow. This is true because
negative attention can be rewarding. If students enjoy
irritating the teacher or causing a disturbance, then
any behavior which accomplishes these goals will probably continue. Forms of negative attention may especially be reinforcing if positive forms of attention are
not made available. Madsen, et al. (1968) have con-
ducted an interesting study relevant to this point
which involved reprimanding children for being out of
their seats. It was found that in a classroom where
students received very little attention for working at
their desks and frequent scolding for out of seat behavior, out of seat activities increased. The reprimands simply reinforced the out of seat behavior. It
was not until the teacher began praising students for
working at their desks and discontinued the reprimands
that sitting and working increased. Sometimes the best
strategy for reducing disruptive behavior is to reinforce behavior which is incompatible with the disruptive response. Students cannot engage in two incompatible responses at the same time. For example, they
cannot sit and stand, talk and be quiet, run and walk,
simultaneously. Strengthening an appropriate response
which is incompatible with disruptive behavior will
automatically reduce the disruptive behavior. This
approach allows teachers to emphasize positive behavior
and indirectly deal with misbehavior. This indirect
method may mean that the teacher must ignore certain

21

minor infractions. Disruptions such as dropping a pencil or speaking out of turn may decrease if they are ignored and do not result in the attention the student desires. Of course withholding attention from all disruptive situations is not possible or desirable. Many of the students' disruptive behaviors will be attended to by classmates and reinforced regardless of the teacher's actions. Other behaviors such as fighting and loud talking are so serious they demand immediate attention. Providing consequences for inappropriate behavior will be addressed later in this chapter.

Finding Other Reinforcers. Have you ever tried reinforcing a student only to find that your efforts failed? Sometimes the things teachers believe will be reinforcing are perceived differently by students. One teacher the author knows used candy. When it did not produce the desired results the teacher became discouraged and concluded that the behavioral approach did not work. Obviously, part of the problem was due to the students' lack of interest in candy as a reinforcer. Teachers cannot always successfully conclude that they know what will work with their students. At times a little exploring is necessary.

One way of determining what serves as a reinforcer is to ask students what they like and what activities they prefer. This may be accomplished in a class discussion where students indicate the activities and things they would enjoy. If you attempt this type of discussion, prepare yourself for some responses which are impossible to implement in a school setting. Although it will not be possible to utilize each suggestion the students make, their discussion should provide a wealth of ideas concerning what they would find reinforcing. Another approach to determining what students find reinforcing is to observe what activities they engage in during free time. What books do they read? What hobbies do they enjoy? Your observations can provide valuable information about possible reinforcers.

Regardless of whether you ask students or observe them during free time, you will soon find that their interests vary. Some like to engage in active play, others read, while still others may prefer to talk with friends. It is valuable to realize that the events which are reinforcing for one student may not be for another. If teachers are to use reinforcement successfully, a variety of reinforcers must be made available.

Using Reinforcers as Consequences. Some positive consequences like praise and attention are best used to reinforce appropriate behavior without specifying the exact conditions necessary for their use. Other positive consequences should be provided only when the student complies with the rules. Currin and Mendler (1980, p. 122) provide the following guidelines for using positive consequences in this way:

1. The criteria for positive consequences must be clearly spelled out so that there is no doubt when they are earned and what the rewards are.

2. The consequences should be attainable.

3. The rewards should be personally meaningful to the student.

4. You can have positive consequences for each rule or for students who do not break any rule. For example: any student who does not interrupt the class for one week can have ten minutes of free time (a consequence for a given rule); any student who does not break any rule for three days receives a weekend with no homework (an all rules consequence).

The importance of providing positive consequences for appropriate behavior cannot be overemphasized. Behaviors are strengthened only through reinforcement.

Some Things to Remember. Properly reinforcing appropriate behavior is not always easy. Some snags and pitfalls sometimes cause teachers to become frustrated and even give up. Some suggestions concerning things to remember may be helpful.

1. Don't overlook appropriate behavior or take it for granted. Rather, find ways to reinforce it.

2. Specify what behavior is appropriate so that students have a clear idea concerning what is expected. Written rules are usually essential if this is to be accomplished.

3. Clearly indicate in writing what positive consequences will result when rules are followed.

4. Reinforcers which teachers believe will be effective may not be perceived in the same way by students. Teachers must be sensitive to how students perceive. Consider asking for your students' suggestions and carefully observing their behavior during free time.

5. The power of a reinforcer may become weakened if used too frequently. On the other hand reinforcers spaced too far apart may not provide the incentive needed to significantly increase behavior. Again, teachers must be good observers and be able to use good judgment concerning what is best.

6. Be consistent in applying reinforcement. If a response is reinforced on one occasion and then punished the next, students become confused. Similarly, if students are rewarded for a behavior and then the behavior is never reinforced again, extinction may gradually occur.

7. Be careful not to reinforce inappropriate behavior. As logical as this appears, it is a frequent pitfall. As we have seen, in some instances paying attention to inappropriate behavior may actually increase its occurrence.

8. Consider reinforcing responses which are incompatible with disruptive behavior. Strengthening the incompatible behavior will reduce the disruptive responses.

9. Certain behaviors may need to be shaped or rewarded in small bits and pieces until the total response is learned. For example, some young children may not be able to sit and work on a task for 30 minutes. It may be best to reinforce these students every five minutes and as you are successful space our reinforcement thereafter. Or instead of telling a student he will be rewarded on Friday if he brings his homework each day during the week, you may, at first, need to provide reinforcement each day homework is prepared. <u>Remember, don't initially expect more than students can deliver</u>. In this regard, careful observation and sensitivity to the student's situation is essential.

10. Keep in mind that while you are strengthening appropriate behavior by providing pleasant consequences, you are also associating yourself, the class and the subject matter with things which help students develop positive feelings and approach tendencies.

Providing Consequences for Inappropriate Behavior

Although some behaviorists believe that effective management can be achieved simply through the use of positive reinforcement, others prefer to combine positive reinforcement with some form of punishment. In the past teachers and school administrators usually thought of only one type of punishment when seeking to alter student behavior--applying such an aversive stimulus that the student would forevermore want to avoid such a consequence. Such stimuli can take the form of spankings, severe criticism and public ridicule. These Type I punishments (adding something aversive to the environment after a response has been made) are still advocated by some parents and school critics. For these individuals a dose of the old-time discipline is needed to get the school back on track. Although treating students in harsh ways may suppress inappropriate behavior, there are many reasons for abandoning such practices. We have already discussed one of these reasons at some length--associating school stimuli with things which automatically produce negative feelings and avoidance tendencies will produce these same feelings and tendencies toward school stimuli. Very few students learn to like school work when it is associated with harsh, aversive conditions. Instead they learn to dislike school, hate the teacher and avoid the subject matter. With such negative feelings and tencencies, negative behavior is usually not far behind. Some students openly act in aggressive ways while others, because of fear, withdraw. Neither response is conducive to learning.

Another reason for caution when considering harsh punishment involves the modeling effect. If teachers or other school personnel serve as aggressive models in dealing with disruptive behavior, students may learn that aggression is appropriate for those who are powerful. Thus, using aggression may actually increase the students' tendency to be aggressive in certain situations. For these reasons most behaviorists prefer other, less harsh methods of suppressing inappropriate behavior. These methods frequently involve removing a positive reinforcer after an inappropriate response has occurred. Undesirable side effects may also result from utilizing mild punishment of this type, although it seems less likely, especially when this method is supplemented with positive reinforcement for appropriate behavior. Kazden (1980, p. 167) discusses three types of punishment procedures which involve a penalty for inappropriate behavior--time out, response cost, and overcorrection.

Time Out. The removal of reinforcement for a specified time period is referred to as time out. If being with the group, talking to friends, or taking part in classroom activities are reinforcing, then the removal of these sources of reinforcement after inappropriate behavior can be viewed as punishment. It must be noted that if time out is to be effective the classroom must be a reinforcing environment. Furthermore, if time out is used the student must be removed from all sources of reinforcement. This is not easily achieved. One teacher sent students to a small room adjacent to the classroom. This room had a window overlooking the playground where students enjoyed watching play and even waving to their friends. Sending the student to this room may have calmed the teacher's nerves but it did not sufficiently allow for an unstimulating environment. At times teachers have partitioned off certain areas of the classroom so that adequate time out space is available and some schools have even designated rooms for this purpose. When considering the use of time out, avoid areas that are frightening, such as dark rooms, and refrain from excluding children for lengthy periods of time. Remember, the goal of time out is to suppress inappropriate behavior by the removal of positive reinforcement, not to scare children or disallow them an education. When children return from time out, teachers should prompt appropriate behavior ("You may start working on your project now") and reinforce these responses when they occur.

Response Cost. Response cost also refers to the loss of positive reinforcement but usually in the form of a fine or loss of privileges. It is similar to a traffic fine for speeding. For breaking the law we must pay a penalty. Clark et al. (1977) discussed an interesting response cost procedure for controlling the behavior of children in the supermarket. The children were each given fifty cents and told that they could spend their money when the parent reached the checkout counter if they had not misbehaved. Misbehavior was defined as running, touching merchandise, etc. However, for every instance of misbehavior, they would be assessed a five cent penalty. The results of this response cost procedure revealed that inappropriate behavior dropped significantly under these conditions when compared with the children's behavior prior to the implementation of response cost. In schools, response cost procedures are especially well suited for systematic behavior management programs such as token economies. In these programs appropriate behavior earns tokens which can be exchanged for back-up reinforcers, i.e., things which are valued by students. At the same time inappropriate behavior results in the loss of tokens and, therefore, the loss of back-up reinforcers. We will discuss systematic approaches to classroom management in a later section of this chapter.

Overcorrection. Another technique which involves a penalty is overcorrection. When this procedure is used the student must positively practice the appropriate behavior and/or restore the environment so that it is better than before the misbehavior. Sometimes it is possible to combine both of these practices. For example, the student who leaves books scattered all over the floor in the library might be required to pick up these books and put them in the proper place, and also shelve other books. Of course for many behaviors which the teacher desires to suppress there is no environmental consequence which can be corrected. When students engage in loud talking or even fighting there may be no consequences to the physical environment. Azren and Powers (1975) used positive practice to control the disruptive behavior of boys in a classroom situation. These boys were required to give up a recess period and practice remaining in their seats and raising their hands to receive attention. After the practice session, there was a decline in their disruptive behavior. It is interesting to note that in this study loss of recess, without positive practice, had no significant effect on disruptive behavior. In some cases teachers may need to combine response cost (i.e., denying privileges) with positive practice if the best results are to be achieved.

Using Punishment as a Consequence. If punishment is utilized its purpose should be to suppress inappropriate behavior, not to get even or hurt students. If inappropriate behavior is no longer occurring it is more likely that appropriate behavior can be encouraged and rewarded. Rules and consequences for violating rules must be clearly stated so that there is no doubt

27

when a rule has been broken and what consequences will result. For example, if two students are caught fighting, one or more of the following consequences might occur. The students must: (1) apologize to the class for fighting, (2) lose free time privileges, (3) spend five minutes in time out. Since the consequences are stated, the students know what to expect.

Frequently teachers ask whether writing statements such as, I must not misbehave in class, or requiring students to stay in at recess, should be used as punishments. Some behaviorists believe that having students write statements over and over and depriving them of recess do not focus attention on the students' greatest need--learning how to comply with the rules. From this viewpoint, it is more appropriate to ask students to discuss with the teacher, or write out for the teacher, ways to improve behavior, and then initiate and reinforce positive practice. This could be done during a recess period and may involve writing, but the focus is positive. The approach has several advantages:

1. It requires the student to initiate ideas concerning how to comply with the rules.

2. It focuses on learning appropriate behavior rather than punishing inappropriate behavior.

3. When appropriate behavior occurs it is reinforced.

4. With the focus on appropriate behavior, students are more likely to perceive the teacher as wanting to help them rather than hurt them.

Some Things to Remember. Just as reinforcing appropriate behavior is not always simple, using punishment effectively can also be difficult. For this reason some suggestions based upon our previous discussion are presented.

1. Be careful not to associate overly harsh punishment with school stimuli. This practice may produce negative feelings and avoidance tendencies toward the school environment.

2. Specify what behavior is appropriate and inappropriate and what the consequences for behavior will be. When punishing inappropriate behavior indicate what responses are

28

being punished.

3. When students misbehave consider using time out, response cost, or overcorrection-- positive practice and restoration of the environment.

4. Combine mild punishment for inappropriate behavior with reward for appropriate behavior. Punishment used alone only suppresses disruptive behavior, it does not increase the frequency of appropriate behavior.

5. Cue or prompt appropriate behavior. For instance, when returning from time out, indicate to the student what behavior is appropriate and then reward this behavior. Also, use cues or prompts before behavior becomes inappropriate. For example, if talking increases present a designated cue, perhaps ringing a bell or flipping a light switch, to prompt appropriate behavior.

6. Be consistent when using punishment. Don't reward or ignore the infraction of a rule one minute and punish it the next.

7. Be aware of how things seem to the student. Consequences which teachers believe to be aversive may not be perceived in this way by some class members. Even paddlings have been viewed positively when peer admiration has been based upon the number of licks one has received.

8. Be calm when dealing with misbehavior. If the goal of students is to make the teacher angry, an emotional outburst may serve to reinforce the misbehavior.

9. Don't take students' misbehavior personally. A student's problems with parents and peers can result in negative attitudes and inappropriate behavior at school.

10. Do not lecture or bargain with a student after inappropriate behavior has occurred. Instead, specifically state the rule which has been violated ("Jimmy, you kicked Ralph; I want you to keep your hands to yourself") and indicate the consequences ("I'm giving you a warning

this time, if it happens again I'm sending you to time out for five minutes").

Combining Reinforcement and Punishment

Dr. Lee Cantor, author of <u>Assertive Discipline</u>, suggests an approach for elementary teachers which combines reward and punishment. Teachers are instructed to specify appropriate behavior and the consequences which will occur when students behave appropriately and inappropriately. He suggests that a chart be used to display the rules and that each student write the rules and keep a copy at his desk. Furthermore, students are asked to write a letter to their parents stating the class discipline policy and the consequences for adhering to and violating the rules. Parents are to sign the letter and return it to the teacher.

To reward appropriate behavior and punish inappropriate behavior, Dr. Cantor offers several suggestions. Students should be informed that the first time someone violates a rule the student's name will be written on the board. This means that the misbehaving child must stay after school for ten minutes. If the child continues to be disruptive the teacher places a check next to the child's name which adds an additional ten minutes to the detention period. If a child has more than two checks during the day the teacher will call the child's parents.

To reward positive behavior the teacher uses a bag of marbles and an empty jar. Periodically, if the class or a student in the class has behaved appropriately, the teacher drops a marble into the jar and states why the class is being rewarded. Each marble dropped into the jar can earn the class various rewards, such as 30 seconds of free time, one minute toward a party or a movie when the jar is completely filled. Dr. Cantor reports that the marble-jar technique used in combination with punishment has been very effective even with difficult classes.

The Systematic Use of Behavior Management in the Classroom

Many teachers find that students want to learn and that it is not difficult to manage students' behavior. These teachers have found an approach which works for them and are able to use rewards and punishments effectively. Other teachers, perhaps due to no fault of their own, find themselves overcome by problems. These problems may be due to students who are unmotivated, negative, or hostile. In this situation controlling students' behavior can become a major obstacle to learning. To manage behavior in this type of classroom, the teacher may want to utilize a very systematic approach to classroom management referred to as contingency contracting. A contingency contract involves an agreement between the teacher and students which states that when students behave appropriately the teacher provides them with something they value. Conversely, it may state that if students behave inappropriately something of value is taken away. The word contingency implies that the consequences which occur depend upon the behavior of the student. While contingency contracting may be helpful for any teacher, it appears to have its greatest usefulness in classrooms where the teacher is struggling with management problems. In a contingency agreement it is important to provide a description of appropriate behavior, inappropriate behavior, and the consequences that will result from appropriate and inappropriate behavior.

Involving the Students. As we have previously mentioned, it may be best to have students involved in determining classroom rules. This also applies to the development of a contingency contract. Many experts believe that teachers need to seek suggestions from students concerning the provisions of the contract. Asking class members a series of questions has proven helpful. "What could be done to make this class a better place to learn?" "What are some of the things students should not do--things which interfere with learning?" Students' ideas could be listed on the board and discussed by the class. The teacher, too, can make suggestions. After developing this list students could discuss the consequences of appropriate and inappropriate behavior. It is best to first direct the attention of the class to possible consequences of appropriate behavior. "What would you like to do in this class that you are not allowed to do?" A starter question like this can get the discussion going. Again, the teacher might want to list suggestions on the board and have the class assess each suggestion. By now you have probably realized that we are again talking about ways of finding effective reinforcers for students, something we discussed in a previous section. Frequently in these discussions suggestions are made which cannot be implemented. Some things are against school rules and others are just impossible to allow in the classroom. Indicating a willingness to listen but at

31

the same time explaining the limitations helps students to realize the teacher is attempting to be serious about providing opportunities for enjoyable activities. With older students, rather than begin with a discussion, the teacher might administer a questionnaire concerning what students perceive to be appropriate, inappropriate, and highly enjoyable behaviors. Then a discussion of the questionnaire results could lead to the development of the contract.

It is important that as the teacher discusses how the rules and the consequences for appropriate and inappropriate behavior will be utilized in a contract, that the emphasis be placed on providing consequences for appropriate behavior. If the teacher explains that appropriate behavior will be enthusiastically rewarded with consequences which have been suggested by the students, perceptions of the new procedure are more likely to be positive.

Developing the Contract. There are many ways to develop a behavioral contract. Agreements can provide for all kinds of provisions concerning appropriate and inappropriate behavior. Each contract should be tailored to the situation and the needs of both teachers and students. The following discussion will provide some information concerning what could be included in a behavioral contract and how contracting might work.

After reaching some agreement concerning what behaviors are appropriate and inappropriate and what consequences should result from behavior, the teacher needs to provide students with this information. Frequently teachers mimeograph copies of the provisions of the contract and either give them to students or display them on the bulletin board where they can easily be seen. Appropriate behavior might include the following:

1. Bringing books and appropriate materials to class such as pencil and paper.

2. Being quiet while the teacher or someone else is talking.

3. Working on class assignments without disrupting others.

4. Raising your hand and being called on before speaking.

5. Taking part in class or group discussions.

6. Completing a work assignment.

Inappropriate behavior might include the following:

1. Talking or laughing which disturbs others or occurs while the teacher or someone else is talking.

2. Hitting or fighting.

3. Throwing objects.

4. Being out of one's seat without permission.

5. Using dirty language or gestures.

Along with the lists of appropriate and inappropriate behavior you will also have a list of privileges which can be used as reinforcers for appropriate behavior. Some privileges used in one sixth grade class included:

1. Playing board games such as checkers, baseball, and football.

2. Reading magazines such as Sports Illustrated, Hot Rod, Seventeen, and Car and Driver. (Note: You might want to contact a magazine distributor to see if old magazines could be donated, or perhaps ask the PTA to collect old magazines for classroom use.)

3. Talking quietly with friends.

4. Reading comic books.

5. Working on crafts such as model airplanes, needlepoint, etc.

In brainstorming sessions students and teachers have come up with some excellent ideas for privileges. One teacher, realizing that some of her boys enjoyed playing a certain football game, was able to provide the game and even other sports games which were equally enjoyable. The girls were given an opportunity to learn cross-stitch, which proved highly reinforcing.

Of course, engaging in appropriate activities is not the only consequence for appropriate behavior.

33

Awards and prizes can also be utilized. Professional football or baseball cards, small pennants, and sports stickers have been found effective. In several of the above instances, the teacher working through the distributor was able to get a special price since these items were to be used in schools. Although these teachers had to spend a small amount of money for the reinforcers, the increase in appropriate behavior and the change in students' attitude made it worthwhile.

Providing Reinforcers. You may have wondered at this point how a teacher dispenses reinforcers, since the things which have been mentioned cannot be provided after each appropriate response. The teacher must have some kind of credit or token system so that these credits can be given after appropriate behavior occurs. The credits then can be used at a later time in exchange for the privileges, activities, and rewards we have mentioned. Many teachers working with older students find that a point system works best. Points are awarded for appropriate behavior and may be taken away for inappropriate behavior. Accumulating a certain number of points allows the student to enjoy one or more of the privileges during a free time period. Free time can be made available at the end of the period or perhaps at the end of the day. If a point system is used the teacher does not need to give students a material object but can verbally communicate messages such as "Timmy gets two points for following directions" or "Bill loses two points for throwing paper." A disadvantage of a point system involves the paperwork necessary to keep track of each student's points. This is a real concern of teachers since they are already overburdened with paperwork. With proper organization, record keeping has not been found to be excessive and overly time-consuming. Utilizing special forms for recording points, tallying points at certain times of the day, and even using student helpers to assist in record keeping makes a point system more manageable. Some teachers have even allowed certain students to keep their own record of points. Others give privileges and free time based on the previous day's behavior in order to reduce the amount of record keeping which must be done at school. For example, on Wednesday students would earn free time if they had accumulated the necessary points on Tuesday. This would allow the teacher to make the point tallies at the end of the day or the night before. With younger students it may be best to use tangible objects such as plastic chips or buttons which can be exchanged for backup reinforcers. Young children have been found to take great pride in being given a button or other object which represents good behavior. In this case the token itself is a powerful reinforcer.

   Putting the Contract in Writing. After deciding what will go into the contract, then it is necessary for the teacher to put in writing the rules and stipulations which apply. The following is an example of a behavioral contract for a 5th grade class.

Fifth Grade Rules and Regulations
Springfield Elementary School
Teacher: Mrs. Todd

Appropriate Behavior	Immediate Consequences
1. Bringing appropriate class materials such as books and paper	3 points possible
2. Completing assigned homework	4 points
If well done and accurate	2 extra points
3. Listening to instructions or lesson without disrupting others	4 points possible
4. Working on class assignment without disrupting others	4 points possible
5. Taking part in class activities or group discussion	3 points possible

Inappropriate Behavior	Immediate Consequences
1. Loud talking or laughing	Lose--2 points
2. Fighting or hitting another student	Lose--2 points
3. Throwing objects	Lose--2 points
4. Being out of seat without permission	Lose--2 points
5. Using dirty language or gestures	Lose--2 points

<u>Consequences for Appropriate Behavior</u>: The accumulation of 15 points during a period will result in several consequences:

1. A 10-minute free time period at the end of the class when students can play games, read magazines and engage in other agreed upon privileges. Free time will be available on specified days.

2. An opportunity for students to participate in a drawing. Prizes will include football cards, small pennants and other rewards from which the winners choose one prize. This activity will occur on specified days.

3. An opportunity for students to choose a "pay-off" from a list of "pay-offs" the class members have indicated would be rewarding, such as having a "good behavior" letter sent home to parents. This will occur on specified days.

- - - - - - -

I agree to abide by the conditions of this contract.

Student signature_____

Teacher signature_____

_____

Most teachers find that they must experiment in order to determine what works best. Some teachers mimeograph a copy of the contract for each student, providing a place for student and teacher to sign, indicating agreement to abide by the terms of the contract. Other teachers print the contract on poster paper and display it on the bulletin board. These teachers may verbally commit to the contract and ask students to do the same. A record of student points is sometimes posted on the bulletin board or plotted on a graph so that students can see their progress. Usually after a specified time period, it is necessary to consult with the class to see if changes need to be made in the agreement. Frequently, both teacher and students are aware of changes which will lead to improvements.

Occasionally teachers ask whether rewards can be contingent upon group behavior. That is, no one is rewarded unless the entire class behaves appropriately or meets some agreed upon standard of behavior. Numerous studies (Packard, 1970; Schmidt and Ulrich,

1969; Hamblin, Hathaway and Wodorski, 1971) show that group contingencies can be effective. If powerful reinforcers are identified, then students may monitor the behavior of other students to assure that rewards will be received. The peer pressure brought about by the group contingency may provide added incentive for appropriate behavior. At first glance a group contingency may be very appealing, but there are dangers inherent in such an approach. If most students behave appropriately but still are unable to receive rewards, then the system may be perceived as unfair and students may become discouraged. Bad feelings between students may even result. These factors should certainly be considered before using a contract based on a group contingency.

Evaluating the Contract. If you were a researcher you might evaluate the effectiveness of the contract system by having observers systematically record appropriate and inappropriate behavior both before and during implementation of the contract (see Case Examples 1-3). For most teachers this is impossible without special assistance. However, the teacher can get a feel for how well the system is working by closely observing student behavior. Has appropriate behavior increased? Has inappropriate behavior decreased? Are students enthusiastic about the system and the reinforcers? Is classroom management easier now than previously? Do you yell and scream at students less frequently? When questionnaires and discussions are used to evaluate the procedure, are student evaluations mostly positive? The responses you and your students give to these kinds of questions will help you determine the effectiveness of the contract system.

Things to Remember When Using a Contract

1. Allow students to help in developing the contract.

2. Determine what behaviors are appropriate and inappropriate.

3. Specify what the consequences for appropriate and inappropriate behavior will be. How many immediate reinforcers, e.g., points, will be given and taken away for appropriate and inappropriate behavior?

4. Decide whether to use points or some other type of immediate reinforcer. How many immediate reinforcers will be needed to receive free time privileges?

5. Find out what kind of back-up reinforcers (free time activities, rewards) students enjoy and determine those which can be made available. Provide a wide variety of activities and rewards and allow students to choose which they prefer. If possible, introduce entirely new reinforcers from time to time. Remember, appropriate behavior will not be strengthened unless the reinforcers you are utilizing are sufficiently strong to motivate students.

6. Attempt to determine if the program is successful.

Summary

The purpose of this chapter has been to demonstrate the practical applications of classical and operant conditioning to classroom management problems. Classical conditioning was discussed with attention being given to the works of Pavlov and Watson. The work of these men and other classical conditioning theorists explains how attitudes and emotional responses can be conditioned to certain stimuli. In the school environment the findings of classical conditioning are best reflected in the following statement: It is the things which happen to a student in the presence of school stimuli which determine whether the student develops a positive or negative attitude toward these stimuli. Some examples were provided to demonstrate that certain actions tend to encourage positive attitudes and approach tendencies toward learning while other actions tend to encourage negative attitudes and avoidance tendencies.

The discussion of classical conditioning was followed by an introduction to operant conditioning. B. F. Skinner's work was presented and important terms were defined. The application of operant conditioning to classroom management was described in detail. The importance of setting the stage for successful management and providing effective consequences for both appropriate and inappropriate behavior were stressed. The chapter concluded with a discussion of how teachers can systematically apply behavior management principles through the use of contingency contracting.

Hawkins, R. P., Shuyter, D. J., and Smith, C. D. "Modification of Achievement by a Simple Technique Involving Parents and Teachers." In M. Harris (Ed.) Classroom Uses of Behavior Modification. Columbus, Ohio: Charles E. Merrill Publishing Company, 1972, pp. 101-119.

Studies show that the teacher working in cooperation with parents can effectively modify a student's behavior. In this study Tim was a fourth grader whose talking out of turn and inattentiveness was a problem to the teacher. Although Tim's academic performance was also poor, the researcher decided to focus on Tim's inattention and inappropriate talking.

In order to determine Tim's rate of inappropriate behavior (talking out of turn and inattention) observers were trained to record Tim's behavior. For thirteen consecutive days during a 20-minute segment of Tim's social studies class, the observers assessed Tim's behavior every ten seconds. The observers marked on a sheet of paper whether Tim did or did not talk out of turn. The same procedure was followed for attention and inattention. Both talking out of turn and inattention were specifically defined so that observers would know precisely how to record behavior.

After determining Tim's rate of inattention and talking out of turn for the 13-day baseline period, the researcher elicited the cooperation of Tim's parents. The parents were told that Tim would receive a note stating, "You did well today in social studies" when his behavior improved enough to meet a certain criterion. The parents agreed to extend Tim's bedtime for one hour whenever he brought home a note. After three notes they agreed to give him a model car and after eight notes another reward was to be given. This reinforcement brought an immediate decrease in Tim's inappropriate behavior. For example, the percentage of intervals in which Tim was observed talking out of turn dropped below 10 percent during the reinforcement period, whereas during baseline the percentage of intervals averaged approximately 30 percent.

The same procedure was used to help Sherry, a fourth grader, improve her academic performance. Sherry was an underachiever in both social studies and arithmetic. During an initial baseline period it was determined that Sherry averaged 37 percent correct in arithmetic and 47 percent correct in social studies. When Sherry's parents were consulted, they agreed to cooperate with the teacher in helping Sherry improve. When Sherry's performance met a specified criterion in either social studies or arithmetic she would be given a note stating, "Sherry did well in arithmetic today" or "Sherry did very well in social studies today." Sherry's parents agreed to give her rewards on those days she brought home a note. They were to praise her for receiving a note and allow her to play outside before dinner if receiving a note for one subject and to play outside before and after dinner if receiving a note for both subjects. On weekends Sherry could play outside only if a certain number of notes had been received during the week. During the reinforcement period, Sherry's grades in both subjects improved dramatically. There were a few days at the beginning of the reinforcement period when Sherry's social studies grade dropped; perhaps because she was testing to see what would happen. When stated consequences were applied, Sherry's performance improved and remained high throughout the remainder of the study. Sherry's performance placed her in the top half of the class in social studies and in the top 10 percent in arithmetic by the end of the 12-day reinforcement period.

CASE EXAMPLE 2-2

Wolf, M., Hansley, E., King, L., Lachowicz, J. and Giles, K. "The Timer Game: A Variable Interval Contingency for the Management of Out of Seat Behavior." In A. Brown and C. Avery (Ed.), Modifying Children's Behavior: A Book of Readings. Springfield, Ill.: Charles C. Thomas Publishers, 1974, pp. 247-253.

Barush, H., Saunders, M., and Wolf, M. "Good Behavior Game: . Effects of Individual Contingencies on Disruptive Behavior in the Classroom." In R. Klien, W. Hapkiewicz, and A. Roden (Ed.), Behavior Modification in Educational Settings. Springfield, Ill.: Charles C. Thomas Publishers, 1973, pp. 230-241.

Games utilizing behavioral principles have been effective in reducing inappropriate behavior. The timer game was used in a class with low achieving third and fourth graders. The children had been working under a token system and were given points for correct answers which could be exchanged for back-up reinforcers, e.g., field trips and snacks. Since getting students to remain in their seats was a problem, the researchers decided that points would also be given for in-seat behavior. This was accomplished by setting a timer that would go off at random intervals during the class period. If a student was in his seat when the timer sounded, he would receive five points. The points earned for in-seat behavior made up only a small portion of the total points a student could earn each day. Nevertheless, the timer game was very effective in reducing out-of-seat behavior. Prior to the introduction of the timer game, observers recorded student in-seat and out-of-seat behavior every 30 seconds and found that on the average each child exhibited 17 intervals containing out-of-seat behavior per class period. With the introduction of the timer game, the average dropped to approximately two intervals per child. When the timer game was then deleted from the point system program, out-of-seat behavior again increased to an average of 17 intervals per child.

. . . . .

In another study, the good behavior game was introduced to reduce the amount of inappropriate talking and out-of-seat behavior in a fourth grade class which had a history of disruption and unmanageable behavior. Prior to the introduction of the game observers marked on a specially prepared sheet the incidence of inappropriate behavior occurring in the class.

41

The observers recorded misbehavior in 60-second intervals. If any student in the class exhibited inappropriate talking or out-of-seat behavior, a mark was made in the proper place indicating that inappropriate behavior had occurred during that interval of time. The recordings were made in both math and reading periods. During the pre-game observation period the median intervals in which inappropriate talking occurred was approximately 96 percent and the median intervals in which out-of-seat behavior occurred was approximately 82 percent.

When the teacher introduced the game, she divided the class into two teams. She then restated the rules and told the class that whenever someone broke a rule a mark would be placed on the chalkboard for that student's team. If a team received the fewest marks or if both teams received fewer than five marks during a class period, the team(s) would get certain privileges. These privileges included wearing victory badges, lining up first or early for lunch, and taking part in a 30-minute free time period at the end of the day. During the time the game was played, out-of-seat behavior and inappropriate talking was significantly reduced. In the math class, the medial intervals scored for inappropriate talking declined to approximately 19 percent and the median intervals scored for out-of-seat behavior declined to approximately 9 percent. Comparable declines were also noted in the reading class. Interestingly, both teams won the game 82 percent of the time.

Ayllon, T., and Roberts, M. D. "Eliminating Discipline Problems by Strengthening Academic Performance." Journal of Applied Behavior Analysis, 7 (1974): 71-76.

Some researchers have suggested that the elimination of discipline problems through the reinforcement of nondisruptive behavior does not lead to an increase in academic performance. Since this argument may have some validity, this study attempts to eliminate discipline problems by rewarding appropriate academic performance. The subjects in the study were drawn from a very disruptive fifth grade class in an urban, upper-middle class school. Since the class was deficient in reading skills, the teacher decided to begin using a contract system for improving reading performance. This performance level was determined each day by the correct answers given to questions involving comprehension, vocabulary, etc., which pertained to the oral group reading activity. A point system was introduced to increase assignment completion rates and performance accuracy. This system allowed students to earn points for improved performance. For example, 100 percent correct on assigned work was worth 5 points and 80 percent correct was worth 2 points. Points could be exchanged for back-up reinforcers such as having access to a game room (2 points), extra recess time (2 points), seeing a movie (6 points) and having a good work letter sent to parents (15 points).

Observers recorded incidents of disruptive behavior for five target students while the reinforcement program was not in effect (baseline), during a reinforcement period which followed the initial baseline, during a second baseline period and during a second reinforcement period.

The results indicated that the reinforcement of academic performance increased reading performance and concurrently reduced disruptive behavior. Both the mean percent of disruptive behavior and the mean performance accuracy rate were in the 40 to 50 percent range during baseline periods. The first reinforcement phase resulted in an increase (to approximately 70 percent) in reading performance and a decrease (to approximately 15 percent) in disruptive behavior. The second baseline period led to a decrease in reading performance rate and an increase in disruptive behavior. When the reinforcement program was reinstated, performance accuracy accelerated to a mean of approximately 85 percent and disruptive behavior decreased to a mean of about 5 percent. The researchers found that the reduction in disruptive behavior which occurred while reading performance was reinforced did not generalize to other academic class periods involving the same teacher, classroom, classmates, etc., leading them to conclude that generalization is unlikely without properly designing its occurrence.

INVOLVEMENT EXERCISES

1. From your own learning experience, what practices can you remember which associated the school, the teacher or the subject matter with aversive conditions?

2. What practices can you remember which associated the school, the teacher or the subject matter with positive conditions?

3. What conditions set the stage for effective classroom management?

4. Why is reinforcement viewed as more effective than punishment in helping students learn to behave in appropriate ways?

5. Explain how negative attention can reinforce inappropriate behavior.

6. Explain how you could use time out, response cost and overcorrection in your classroom.

7. Give two examples of how you could decrease inappropriate behavior by reinforcing a response which is incompatible with the inappropriate response.

8. Stacy is your most disruptive fifth grader. He frequently engages in loud talking, pushing and shoving matches and other out-of-seat behavior. You have decided to combine mild punishment for inappropriate behavior with rewards for appropriate behavior as you deal with Stacy. Specify in what way you will implement this approach.

9. During the first week of class you work with your students to develop some reasonable rules. You now must write these rules so that they are clearly understood and students know when they have violated or conformed to the rules. Using three rules as examples, write these rules so that students will know when they violate or conform to the rules and what consequences will result when violation or conformity occurs.

10. How can you determine if a contingency contract is effective?

11. You have decided to find out what your students find reinforcing. How can you go about determining the reinforcers which will be effective?

12. Write a simple contingency contract for the class you are teaching or will teach. Assume that your students have helped you develop the terms of this contract. Specify the following: appropriate and inappropriate behavior, consequences of behavior, immediate reinforcers, back-up reinforcers, the number of immediate reinforcers necessary to obtain back-up reinforcers.

REFERENCES

Azrin, N. H. and Powers, M. A. "Eliminating classroom disturbances of emotionally disturbed children by positive practice procedures." Behavior Therapy, 1975, 6, 525-534.

Clark, H. B., Green, B. F., Macrae, J. W., McNees, M. P., Dovis, J. L. and Risley, T. R. "A parent advice package for family shopping trips: Development and evaluation." Journal of Applied Behavior Analysis, 1977, 10, 605-624.

Curwin, Richard L. and Mendler, Allen N. The discipline book: A complete guide to school and classroom management. Reston, VA: Reston Publishing Company, 1980.

Hamblin, R. I., Hathaway, C., and Wodarski, M. "Group contingencies, peer tutoring and accelerating academic achievement." In E. A. Ramp and B. L. Hopkins (Eds.), A new direction for education: Behavior analysis. Lawrence: University of Kansas, Department of Human Development, 1971, 41-53.

Kazdin, Alan E. Behavior modification in applied settings. Homewood, IL: The Dorsey Press, 1980.

Madsen, C. H., Jr., Becker, W. C., Thomas, D. R., and Kosen, L. "An analysis of the reinforcing function of 'sit down' commands." In R. K. Parker (Ed.) Readings in educational psychology. Boston: Allyn and Bacon, 1968.

Madsen, Charles, and Madsen, Clifford. Teaching/Discipline: A positive approach for educational development. Boston: Allyn and Bacon, 1974.

Mager, Robert F. Developing attitude toward learning. Palo Alto, CA: Fearon Publishers, 1968.

Packard, R. G. "The control of classroom attention: A group contingency for complex behavior." Journal of Applied Behavior Analysis, 1970, 3, 13-28.

Schmidt, G. W. and Ulrich, R. E. "Effects of group contingent events upon classroom noise." Journal of Applied Behavior Analysis, 1969, 2, 171-79.

Skinner, B. F. About behavior. New York: Knopf,
     1974.

Skinner, B. F. Beyond freedom and dignity. New York:
     Knopf, 1971.

Skinner, B. F. "How to teach animals." Scientific
     American, 1951, 185, 26-29.

Skinner, B. F. Science and human behavior. New York:
     Macmillan, 1953.

Watson, J. B., and Rayner, R. "Conditioned emotional
     reaction." Journal of Experimental Psychology,
     1920, 3, 1-4.

Williams, Robert L., and Anandam, Kamola. Cooperative
     classroom management. Columbus, Ohio: Charles E.
     Merrill, 1973.

CHAPTER 3

THE REALITY ORIENTATION TO
CLASSROOM MANAGEMENT

The reality orientation to classroom management is associated with the work of William Glasser. Dr. Glasser is a psychiatrist who is responsible for developing a new approach to therapy and introducing some innovative ideas concerning the management of schools. In 1965 Glasser published the book Reality Therapy: A New Approach to Psychiatry, in which he outlined his proposals for therapy, and in 1969 his book Schools Without Failure applied his reality orientation to school settings. Dr. Glasser's ideas have been well received by educators and he has spent much of his time helping teachers and administrators implement his proposals. In order to help you understand Glasser's approach, it is necessary to examine reality therapy and the beliefs which led to the development of this approach.

During Glasser's psychiatric training he began to reject the traditional beliefs concerning therapy: the belief that mental illness actually exists, the belief that a patient's past experience and unconscious mind must be understood, and the belief that a patient must gain insight into the dynamics of his personality. Dr. Glasser believed that therapy based on these assumptions did not help patients change. It was even possible that such treatment was harmful since it gave patients good reasons for being troubled and unable to come to grips with their problems.

The Development of Reality Therapy

The rejection of the traditional psychiatric beliefs led to the development of reality therapy. According to Glasser (1965), individuals who need counseling help are not sich but are failing to satisfy two important needs--the need to love and to be loved and the need to feel worthwhile. All humans satisfy these needs through a relationship with someone else. The relationship must be a warm, caring relationship in which another person exhibits his concern through involvement. Parents usually help children fulfill these needs by caring for them and doing the things which are needed to communicate love and a sense of worth. When parents fail in this responsibility, their

49

children may eventually end up needing professional help. Individuals who are unable to satisfy their needs for love and worth exhibit unrealistic behavior in an attempt to compensate. For instance, they may break the law, drink excessively, exhibit excessive fear and anxiety or even experience hallucinations and delusions.

These behaviors may attract attention but they do not involve patients with other people in ways which satisfy their basic needs for love and worth. When individuals are unsuccessful in satisfying the basic needs, they begin to deny reality. Their behavior becomes unrealistic in the sense that it further alienates them from establishing relationships which would lead to the love and worth of others which they so desperately need. The goal of reality therapy is to help patients face the world in a realistic manner and to resolve problems in ways which lead to the satisfaction of the needs for love and worth. Those individuals fortunate enough to fulfill these basic needs are much more likely to behave in responsible ways. Responsibility is defined as "the ability to fulfill one's needs, and to do so in a way that does not deprive others of the ability to fulfill their needs" (1965, p. 13). Reality therapy, then, is directed toward providing a relationship which helps patients satisfy their needs for love and worth and teaches them to behave in responsible ways.

The Involvement of the
Reality Therapist

The first task of the reality therapist is to become involved with the patient. Glasser believes that the therapist's ability to get involved is the most important skill needed to implement this approach. Although involvement is difficult to describe, it concerns the ability of the therapist to care about the patient and to communicate this sense of caring. The reality therapist must feel with the patient but refrain from expressing sympathy for the patient or communicating the idea that irresponsible behavior is justified. At times the therapist must even watch the patient suffer if suffering in the end leads to responsible behavior.

The result of involvement is to show the patient that the therapist cares enough to expect and demand that the patient change. The therapist cares so much that he cannot allow patients to make excuses, blame others or play helpless instead of accepting responsibility for their behavior. There is no magic formula for creating involvement. It takes a caring attitude, a firm belief in the ability of the patient to be responsible, and time. How much time depends upon individual circumstances, but Glasser believes that the next step in the therapeutic process cannot be successful if involvement is not experienced by both the patient and the therapist.

Focusing on Behavior

As involvement occurs, patients must be helped to look at reality; the reality of their own behavior and the consequences of this behavior. Thus, in reality therapy, attention is directed to the patient's behavior. "What are you doing?" is a question frequently asked by the therapist. Patients may have trouble relating this question to their behavior. Some respond by talking about feelings (e.g., "I'm depressed," "angry" or "afraid"). Some patients respond by focusing on the behavior of others (e.g., "they're mistreating me," "spying on me," or "making my life difficult"). To allow the patient to blame others or to continue to concentrate on feelings is nonproductive. In reality therapy the behavior of the patient is emphasized, not the patient's feelings or the behavior of others. If patients are to be helped they must look at what they are doing and evaluate its effectiveness in helping them. Having patients focus on their behavior (e.g., "I've been crying a lot," "I've been staying home from work," "I've been stealing," "I've been taking drugs") stresses the patient's responsibility for this behavior and the need to change if things are going to get better.

Evaluating Behavior

Once the patient is able to talk in terms of his own behavior, he is then asked to evaluate this behavior. "How is your behavior helping you?" Glasser believes that most patients realize that their behavior is deviant and that it is not helping them. After all, if their behavior was acceptable they would not find themselves in need of help. This assessment of behavior on the part of the patient is crucial. Patients must see that their behavior is irresponsible or eventually leave therapy. This is because they cannot be helped until they are willing to honestly evaluate their behavior. The reality therapist believes that after the therapist and patient become involved, most patients will assess their behavior as irresponsible. This will not happen, however, if involvement has not been established. So again, we see the importance of involvement.

Planning to Change

After the patient has evaluated his behavior, the therapist then helps the patient develop a plan to change. Both the patient and therapist may suggest courses of action. Then the patient must implement whatever plan is agreed upon. The following plan involving a patient who had been absent from work for a week because of depression will serve as an example. The patient agreed to:

1. Get up in the mornings at 7 a.m., get dressed, shave, and eat breakfast.

2. Get to work on time and work the entire 8-hour shift.

3. Continue this schedule for one week.

4. Report back to the therapist at the end of the week.

In this case the patient made and signed a written commitment. Although putting a plan in writing may not always be necessary, it is frequently helpful because the patient then knows precisely what behaviors are involved in the commitment. As patients succeed at implementing their plans, further plans may be drawn up if they are needed. Implementing plans teaches the patient to behave responsibly, which should lead to improved relationships with others and a better chance of satisfying the needs for love and worth. Not all patients can learn to be responsible after making just one commitment. Learning responsibility can be difficult for individuals who have consistently denied reality and failed to satisfy their needs for love and worth. If the patient is unsuccessful in carrying out a plan, the therapist does not punish, blame, or accept excuses. To punish or to blame would reinforce the patient's failure and sense of worthlessness. To allow excuses would permit the patient to transfer responsibility to something or someone other than himself. The therapist must continue to focus on the patient's behavior. "You did not carry out the plan. Let's talk about it. Do you want to try again or develop another plan? I'm still concerned about your behavior."

Regardless of how many times patients fail to carry
out plans, the reality therapist continues to be willing to help them try again in their effort to become
responsible.

A Review of Important Terms

* Basic Psychological Needs: The two basic psychological needs are "the need to love and to be
  loved and the need to feel that we are worthwhile
  to ourselves and to others" (1965, p. 9). These
  needs must be fulfilled if an individual is to
  be responsible.

* Responsibility is defined as "the ability to fulfill one's needs and to do so in a way that does
  not deprive others of the ability to fulfill their
  needs" (1965, p. 13).

* Reality is a term which refers to the consequences
  of an individual's behavior as it relates to the
  satisfaction of basic needs. Drinking excessively
  may be unrealistic in the sense that it denies the
  reality of the world, i.e., the fact that the
  person will feel bad later, may lose his job, and
  hurt his wife and family. This irresponsible behavior decreases the chances of adequately satisfying the needs for love and worth. Reality
  therapy continually focuses attention on the
  patient's tendency to deny reality by asking
  "What are you doing?" and "How is it helping you?"

* The goal of reality therapy is to help individuals
  behave in responsible ways, i.e., ways which lead
  to the healthy satisfaction of the needs for love
  and worth.

* Involvement is the word used to describe the relationship which must exist between the patient and
  the therapist if therapy is to be successful.

Summarizing: Things to Remember

1. Reality therapy emphasizes the importance of
   personal involvement between the patient and
   therapist.

2. Reality therapy focuses on the present and
   present behavior rather than on unconscious
   processes and past experience. Although the
   past has affected us, understanding the

influence of the past will not help us change our present behavior.

3. Reality therapists do not emphasize feelings. Although they do not deny that individuals have feelings, they believe that to concentrate on feelings throughout the therapeutic process postpones behavioral change. It is when behavior changes that individuals begin to feel better about themselves and are more likely to satisfy their basic needs for love and worth.

4. The reality therapist asks the patient to evaluate his behavior and believes that the patient, after a period of involvement with the therapist, can see that his behavior is not helping him. It is only after the patient evaluates his behavior that positive change can occur.

5. Reality therapy stresses responsibility and attempts to teach patients to make realistic plans to change their behavior.

6. After a plan has been developed, it is important for the patient to make a commitment to carry out the plan. When plans are implemented, the patient begins to gain maturity and develop a sense of worth.

7. Reality therapy does not punish or accept excuses when patients fail to honor commitments. Punishment would reinforce failure and harm the therapeutic relationship. Allowing excuses would only teach irresponsibility by helping the patient avoid the real truth: that "he is responsible for his behavior" (1965, p. 27).

The Application of Reality Therapy in Institutional Settings

Reality Therapy with Mental Patients. In the book Reality Therapy, Dr. Glasser describes the use of his approach in two institutional settings: the Ventura School for delinquent girls in California and the Veterans Administration Neuropsychiatric Hospital in Los Angeles. Prior to the application of reality therapy principles on a chronic psychotic ward at the V.A. hospital, care of the patients was largely

54

custodial with an average of only two patients being discharged each year. After implementing Glasser's approach, changes in patients' behavior was soon evident. On a ward where 210 patients averaged 17 years of hospitalization, 14 were released the first year, 85 the second, and 90 the third (Glasser and Zunin, 1973, p. 289). A similar success story was occurring at the Ventury School for Girls, where Glasser served as consulting psychiatrist. Before discussing the application of reality therapy to school settings, it will be helpful to see how the reality orientation was implemented at the Ventura School.

Reality Therapy with Delinquents. At Ventura the 400 girls, aged 14 to 21, are not viewed as mentally ill; instead, their behavior is seen as irresponsible. The girls transferred by the state to the Ventura School have all broken the law; some are there for minor offenses while others have been convicted of first degree murder. Most all of the girls have been in and out of juvenile homes but have not seemed to profit from any help which has been offered them. The Ventura School has strict rules and high standards of discipline. Glasser concludes that "unless we have high standards, the students conclude that we are 'phony' and don't care for them" (1965, p. 32). After the girls realize that the rules are enforced consistently and fairly, they learn to understand that "real care is implied by discipline" (1965, p. 72). The girls are rewarded for attending school and taking part in the various aspects of the Ventura program. Irresponsibility, reflected in uncooperative behavior, is not tolerated and results in exclusion from the regular Ventura program. This is not viewed as punishment since it is not done to hurt the girls and does not threaten or inflict pain. Exclusion involves removing the girls from their regular living quarters and school classroom to special quarters where they must remain until they exhibit enough responsibility to return to the regular program. Even in detention all of the physical needs of the girls are met and counselors trained in reality therapy work with them to show their concern and involvement. The regular program is made interesting and attractive so that the girls will want to return to their regular living quarters and school classroom.

The treatment, then, at Ventura applies the following principles of reality therapy:

1. The girls are taught that they are responsible for their own behavior. Blaming others and excusing behavior because of parental neglect, mistreatment and abuse is not helpful. These responses are accepted uncritically by the staff but it is made clear that while the girls are at Ventura they must become responsible for their own behavior regardless of past conditions.

2. Rules are enforced since not to enforce rules would communicate a noncaring attitude. The girls are expected to attend school and cooperate with the other girls and staff members.

3. Involvement is essential to the success of the program. If the girls are to change they must believe that someone cares enough to expect them to do better. Most girls stay at Ventura for six to eight months, which allows staff members enough time to develop a caring involvement in their relationship with the girls.

4. The counselors frequently work with the girls in groups. The verbal interaction that takes place in these groups focuses on behavior and new ways of handling difficult situations.

5. The girls are asked to evaluate their behavior, plan a new course of action, and commit to their plan.

6. If girls fail to behave in a responsible way or do not carry out plans, the staff does not give up. They realize that it can take time to develop responsibility. Excuses for failure are not accepted and no punishment is utilized.

No adolescent rehabilitation program has an easy task. The girls at Ventura are often antagonistic, hostile, and unmotivated to change. The goal is to rehabilitate the girls within six to eight months, although some of the more difficult girls stay longer. Glasser reports (1965, p. 68) that the program is successful with about 80 percent of the girls. This would certainly seem to be a very high success rate and appears to be even more remarkable when compared to other programs. Since writing about the reality therapy approach at Ventura many programs for juvenile offenders throughout the United States have adopted a reality therapy approach.

Teaching Children to Be Responsible

It is not just psychotics and juvenile delinquents who need to learn how to behave in responsible ways. All of us need this help in order to live more productive lives and to avoid the consequences of irresponsible behavior. Unfortunately, there are no programs which exist specifically to teach responsibility. Of course, one might suggest that this is the job of parents. Probably no one would disagree with this suggestion, but it is obvious that many parents are unable to behave in responsible ways themselves. The consequences of poor parenting can be disastrous. Glasser believes that "people who are not at some time in their lives, preferably early, exposed intimately to others who care enough about them both to love and discipline them will not learn to be responsible" (1965, p. 16). Children who have not been able to fulfill their needs for love and worth may have trouble adhering to reasonable rules as well as cooperating with and trusting other people. These children, not being able to satisfy their own needs for love and worth, frequently behave in ways which deprive others of the ability to fulfill needs. When this happens in schools, discipline problems become prevalent as children in their unsuccessful attempts to fulfill their needs act in ways which make it more difficult for other students to behave appropriately.

Since behaving responsibly is not innate but must be learned, the school must share some of the burden for teaching responsibility. In the early 1960's, Glasser taught a university course for school personnel. In this course he attempted to help teachers and administrators deal with the irresponsible behavior of students. In 1966, Glasser began working in elementary schools located in the Watts area of Los Angeles, where he introduced some modifications of reality therapy. These experiences helped Glasser formulate his ideas concerning how reality therapy could be applied to the school environment.

Reality Therapy and the Schools

Although teachers can successfully apply the principles of reality therapy in the classroom, Glasser believes that "the cumulative effect of a whole school using these principles will be much greater in reducing the number of irresponsible children who will need more extensive care later on" (1965, p. 165). Ideally, then, all school personnel would implement a reality approach.

Since adopting the reality orientation on a schoolwide basis is not always possible, each teacher may need to decide what aspects of this approach can be used in the classroom to teach responsibility and improve classroom management. Glasser makes several suggestions which he urges schools to implement.

Basic Needs. Since students must learn to fulfill their needs for love and worth, the school must be an environment which encourages and facilitates the satisfaction of these needs. If children are successful in fulfilling their needs they develop a success identity. These children are loved. They can reach out to others and their feelings of worth are high. It is essential that the school environment be a place where children are given "a chance to give and receive love and a chance to become educated and therefore worthwhile" (1969, p. 14). On the other hand, children who are unable to satisfy their needs for love and worth develop a failure identity. The role of the school is to help children develop success identities rather than failure identities.

Many schools do more to reinforce failure than to encourage success. Glasser believes that most children, regardless of home background, initially come to school in kindergarten or first grade with expectations for success. They have enjoyed learning up to this point and they expect to continue to learn at a rapid rate. If the school sets up roadblocks on every hand, dishes out failure and stifles creativity, children soon wonder why learning is no longer enjoyable. The years from five to ten are critical. Children continue to be somewhat confident during elementary school regardless of school experience. However, if failure continues to be a crucial part of a child's experience during these years, then by age ten that confidence is replaced by a feeling of failure. Children with failure identities rely on emotions rather than logic in their attempt to satisfy their needs for love and worth. Some become desperate and engage in delinquent behavior or withdraw from learning activities. Since a failure identity can be more easily reversed during the early years, Glasser emphasizes the importance of the elementary school. This is not to say that school personnel should give up on older students. The reality orientation advocates believe that an individual can be helped at any age, but that students are more easily helped while they are young and still confident in their ability to satisfy their needs for love and worth.

Memorization. Prior to coming to school the child has experienced a world which has required thinking. In school the child is mostly required to memorize facts and repeat these facts on tests. While this is especially true of the upper grades, it is also true to a certain extent in the lower grades, even beginning in the first grade. The child, expecting school to be stimulating, is confronted with the task of memorizing a vast number of boring, irrelevant facts. Children from the middle and upper class can often survive the shock of a school system which equates learning with memorization. These children have encouragement and help from home and even though they are bored, they plod on and experience some success. Children without this parental support have nothing to fall back on and are doomed to failure. For these children, school becomes a frustrating experience, providing very little satisfaction and sense of accomplishment. Unsuccessful students begin to feel hopeless, alone, and unable to compete in a world of memorization and facts. They begin to act out their problems or withdraw in their attempt to cope. To keep this from happening, schools must change. Glasser believes that thinking must be restored to a place of central importance.

Objective Tests and the Certainty Principle. Consistent with the belief that memorization is detrimental, the reliance on objective tests is also viewed as harmful. Glasser believes that schools are dominated by the certainty principle. This is the idea that every question has a right answer. This philosophy leads to an educational system that programs students to regurgitate right answers. Such a system ignores the importance of free discussion and denies the student an opportunity to grapple with many intriguing and relevant questions. So prevalent is the certainty principle that many children do not understand that there are questions which do not have right answers.

Since schools are dominated by the certainty principle and a reliance on memorization, tests are passed by memorizing facts and knowing right answers rather than exhibiting an ability to use essential facts in the thinking process. Frequently, teachers who give

59

right answer, objective type tests utilize the normal curve to determine what grades students receive. This is a sure way to reduce students' motivation. It allows only a few to get A's and B's while many are labeled failures. Glasser believes that if tests requiring fact only information are given, they should be used for self-evaluation and not for grading purposes. If thinking is an important goal, a more sensible approach to testing would be the use of open book examinations. These exams teach students to use facts in solving problems and to use and understand the importance of reference material. This is realistic since life teaches us to look up information rather than committing everything to memory.

The certainty principle not only dominates the curriculum but also permeates the schools' rules and regulations. Glasser believes that students should be allowed to take part in the development of both the rules and the school curriculum. If democracy is going to be relevant to students they must participate in decision-making and understand that rules can be modified.

The Grading System. The reality orientation with its stress on thinking rather than memorization advocates abolishing the traditional A-F grading system. This system emphasizes failure which is at the root of many of the students' problems. Glasser suggests that "no student ever at any time be labeled a failure or led to believe he is a failure through the use of the grading system" (1969, p. 95). Students who are labeled failures stop working. This increases their chances of more failure and eventually results in the development of a failure identity. The school must communicate to students that as far as grades or labels are concerned, no one can fail at school. Although there are many arguments for the use of the traditional grading system, advocates of the reality orientation believe that the harm done by the system far outweighs the good.

To replace the traditional A-F system, Glasser suggests that in the first six grades every student pass each year. This means that the traditional report card is not needed since no student fails. In order to communicate to parents, the teacher should periodically provide written statements which focus in a positive way on the child's progress and areas of needed improvement. In order to encourage students who are motivated to do extra work on their own, an S (superior) is given when students take responsibility for extra work, plan their effort, set their own standards and, in the judgment of the teacher, produce superior work. An S can be given in only one subject area each semester and should represent considerable work in an area which the student has defined as relevant.

In secondary schools the suggested grading system is very similar. No one is given a failing grade. Students are given P (Pass) or no grade, which indicates that a student did not complete the course and meet the teacher's established criteria. No failing mark is recorded in a student's record. A student may repeat a course; however, after taking a course twice, the student must appeal to a faculty committee before enrolling again. The grade of S is used in the same manner as in elementary school.

Because some students in high school may pass only a few college preparatory courses, Glasser suggests that several alternatives to the college bound program be offered. These would include vocational and skill courses and would allow students who otherwise might not succeed to continue learning in an area which is appropriate to their needs.

Ability Grouping. The present practice of homogeneous grouping by ability should be replaced in the elementary school by classes grouped only by age. As students progress through junior high and high school a natural grouping will occur as some students choose more difficult subjects than others. This is to be expected and is different from arbitrarily grouping in terms of ability. In elementary schools where homogeneous grouping is most prevalent, its debilitating effect is seen in teachers as well as students. Teachers assigned to teach the lower groups often resent the assignment and may even come to view the students in a very negative way. This attitude on the part of the teacher makes it even more difficult for these students to succeed. In the end you have students and teachers placed in an environment which neither likes but both must tolerate because someone has concluded that this is the way education works best. To avoid this dilemma, schools should place both low ability students and disruptive students as evenly as possible throughout their respective grades. The only exception to this is in the area of reading. In cases where there is both a wide range of reading abilities and many disruptive students, homogeneous reading classes in which students are grouped by ability may be necessary in order to keep both students and teachers from becoming discouraged. If these two conditions (a wide range of reading abilities and many disruptive students) do not exist, then grouping by age is preferable. Since reading problems and behavioral problems are not usually severe in the first two grades, homogeneous reading groups are not needed at these levels.

The overall purpose of grouping children by age rather than by ability is to prevent children from viewing themselves as failures: abandoned to the dump heap of the lower track class. Initially, classes grouped solely by age may be harder to teach, but as teachers adjust they will find that with fewer children believing themselves to be failures, teaching becomes easier. Students also benefit by having to communicate with all types of peers and by realizing that everyone is worthy of respect.

Curriculum. With an emphasis on memorization of facts and right answers, schools have failed to make learning relevant. Students frequently cannot see how the things they memorize in school have any meaning for their lives. Since an irrelevant curriculum interferes with a student's motivation to learn, the subject matter must be related to something children do outside the school environment. This takes some effort but it is necessary so that students will not conclude that education is a waste of time. Since relevance is frequently not apparent, teachers must teach relevance by relating subject matter to the real concerns of students.

In some cases even teachers cannot see the relevance of subject matter. When this happens, perhaps the curriculum can be changed. If not, it is best to be honest and explain to students that it is unclear why this material is part of the curriculum; nevertheless, you are required to teach it anyway.

Furthermore, school material must be made exciting and realistic. This helps to bridge the relevance gap since those things which sustain children's interest and attention are things which are important in their day-to-day lives. In-class activities should include responses which children find enjoyable in other settings. Glasser believes that "laughter, shouting, loud unison responses, even crying are a part of any good learning experience and should be heard from every class" (1969, p. 56).

Another aspect of making school relevant involves allowing students to discuss their interests, ideas, feelings and opinions at school. Students must realize that the feelings and opinions they have outside of school have a place in education. Educators must reduce the emphasis on right answers and allow students the opportunity to explore their feelings and opinions as they think through issues which are important to them. In the next section, we will see how Glasser believes this can be accomplished.

An Interim Summary

Before we go further, let us review what has been said in this chapter. Glasser became disillusioned with the traditional psychiatric approach to helping people. He began experimenting with new ideas and methods. This led to the belief that man has two essential needs beyond the physiological needs. These are the need to love and to be loved and the need for worth. If an individual fulfills these needs he develops a success identity. If these needs go unfulfilled the individual develops a failure identity. An individual with a failure identity behaves in irresponsible ways in attempting to satisfy the needs for love and worth. He is lonely and desperate and in his desperation he fails to use logic and reason to satisfy his needs. Instead, he relies more on emotion, which frequently leads to more irresponsible behavior. In working with patients and with delinquent girls at the Ventura School in California, Glasser established an approach based on the concept of responsibility. At Ventura the girls were shown love by providing an environment characterized by caring and discipline. The staff became involved with them to the extent that the girls realized, perhaps for the first time, that someone cared enough about them to expect their behavior to be responsible. This concern along with other reality oriented procedures such as emphasizing present behavior rather than the past, taking responsibility for one's own behavior and making and carrying out realistic plans, led to a high success rate with the girls. Glasser then began to apply reality therapy to other institutions which were struggling with the problem of helping people become more responsible. He worked in schools and taught courses for teachers which provided the groundwork for the application of his ideas in school settings. Glasser concluded that many schools engage in practices which contribute to the development of a failure identity rather than a success identity. In order to become more effective schools must begin to emphasize thinking rather than memorization, change the traditional A-F grading system, avoid the use of objective tests for determining grades, group students by age, not ability, and make school and the subject matter more relevant to the lives of students. By doing these things schools will become more effective at helping students satisfy their needs for love and worth.

The Teacher and the Reality Orientation

The emphasis in this discussion has been on the practices which schools engage in that are harmful to students. Although changes which need to be made have been mentioned (e.g., providing more relevance), our attention has not yet focused on how to implement these changes. We will do so in this section. Also, you may be wondering how the ideas of reality therapy specifically relate to classroom management. Hopefully this will become much more apparent as you continue to read this chapter. One more point needs to be made here. Individual teachers, acting alone, cannot bring about all the changes which Glasser suggests. This kind of reorganization involves cooperation between teachers, administrators, school board members and the community. Even though it would be best to institute these ideas on a schoolwide basis, when this is impossible teachers can effectively made use of certain aspects of this approach. For this reason, it is hoped that the reader will not despair if full implementation of these ideas is not feasible, but rather, read on with the intention of learning how to use those ideas which can be implemented. Many teachers, working in this way, have utilized Glasser's suggestions to help them manage students' behavior and at the same time help students become more responsible.

Applying a Reality Orientation
in the Classroom

Classroom Meetings. If you recall, the first step of reality therapy is to become involved. For teachers, this means that they must communicate a concern and sense of caring for their students. Certainly most teachers have this concern; however, they may believe that it is improper to exhibit an involvement which reflects concern or, perhaps, they do not know how to effectively communicate concern. The reality orientation suggests that for the purpose of creating an involvement with students and making school more relevant for students, that teachers institute classroom meetings. These meetings should be a regular part of the curriculum and it is suggested that they occur "at least once a day in elementary school and perhaps two or three times a week in high school" (1969, p. 143). These meetings are different from regular discussions because the class members are not searching for right answers, but rather exploring feelings, opinions and ideas as they are stimulated to think.

As you read about class meetings, remember one of their major purposes is to allow the teacher to show concern for students through involvement. In reality therapy if involvement does not exist between patient and therapist, the patient does not believe you care about him and thus resists change. In the classroom, involvement is equally important. If students do not sense your concern for their interests, feelings, and opinions, then it will be more difficult to help them become responsible. Class meetings also made education relevant, convince students that their contributions are important and elevate thinking to a place of importance.

There are three types of classroom meetings. Open-ended meetings address intellectually stimulating subjects. Education-diagnostic meetings address students' understanding of concepts which are a part of the curriculum. Social-problem-solving meetings address concerns about social behavior.

Open-ended Meetings. The open-ended class meeting is designed to allow discussion of any thought-provoking question which students or teachers want to discuss with the class. These meetings are the basis for relevant education since they give students an opportunity to explore questions which they find interesting. Remember, in these discussions right answers are not important. It is the stimulation of thinking about relevant questions which serves as the central focus.

On one occasion when an open-ended meeting was used, a second grade class arrived at school and noticed that the roof in their classroom was leaking. This excited the students and some of the boys even wanted to stand under the leak to see if they could get wet. The teacher seized on this interest and brought up the leaking roof during the open-ended discussion that day. "Why was the roof leaking? After all, the sun had been shining all day." One child thought a pipe must have broken and another felt that perhaps someone was on the roof pouring water through a hole. Through a series of questions, the teacher was able to direct their attention to a number of factors. "What shape was the roof?" "Was it like the roof on a house?" "What was the difference?" Realizing that the roof was flat, someone mentioned that it was just like a table top and if you poured water on a table top it would not all run off immediately. By this time most everyone was eager to get into the discussion and many ideas were suggested, including the idea that perhaps it had rained during the night and water had accumulated on the flat roof and was slowly leaking into the classroom. This discussion took about 15 minutes, everyone was eager to contribute and no answer was criticized. The students seemed to feel good, as if they were unraveling a mystery, and in the process they learned something about free discussion and the process of thinking. As this example indicates, any subject is fair game for the open-ended discussion as long as the children want to talk about the subject and perceive it to be related to their lives.

Educational-Diagnostic Meetings. Educational-diagnostic meetings are always related to the content of the curriculum. The subjects discussed usually pertain to topics which the students have been studying and can frequently allow teachers to assess the effectiveness of their teaching. In one fifth grade class the students had been studying the American Revolution. When they were asked why the American Revolution was fought they tended to give the correct textbook type answers such as "to insure freedom." When asked what freedom was, one girl responded by saying, "It's when you can do what you want to do." This led to a broader discussion of freedom involving the following questions: Are you free? What limits are placed on your freedom? Are there any countries in the world where people are not free? Was freedom worth fighting for? Would it be worth fighting for today? As you can imagine, many of these and the other related questions discussed were difficult for the students to grapple with in an intellectual way. However, since they seemed sufficiently interested, the subject of freedom was the focus of several educational-diagnostic meetings. The questions relevant to class meetings are perceived quite differently by students when compared to the typical right and wrong answer questions. These open-ended questions teach students that when issues related to subject matter are acted upon through thought, the issues not only become stimulating but the subject matter and facts themselves take on new meaning.

<u>Social-Problem-Solving Meetings</u>. The social-problem-solving meeting is used to discuss problems that occur when students interact with each other or have trouble conforming to the rules. Presently when these problems exist there is no forum for students to discuss their difficulties. Instead, they are left to work things out the best they can. With little help from adults, children use strategies which are nonproductive. Fighting, lying, denying behavior and blaming someone else are examples. These strategies do not teach children to rationally approach the problems of interpersonal relationships. The purpose of the social-problem-solving meeting is to involve students in a rational approach to interpersonal problem-solving. In these meetings anyone may suggest a problem for discussion. A student may want to talk about an incident on the playground, the teacher may want to discuss the violation of a rule or the principal may want the class to talk about how new students can make friends. Any problem is relevant to these discussions if it pertains to the class or any member of the class. Sometimes children want to bring up problems of a personal nature that relate to their home life. Generally adults do not openly discuss problems of this kind, rather they avoid exposing the problem or struggle with it privately. Glasser believes that children do not find such discussions so difficult.

In social-problem-solving meetings the direction of the discussion should be toward a solution, never toward punishment or placing blame. If Johnny pushed Sally, the emphasis should be on how Johnny can behave better in the future. Why Johnny pushed Sally or determining whose fault it was is not important. What Johnny did is important. It is not easy at first for children to focus on their behavior. Like adults, they sometimes want to deny their behavior or blame others. Getting Johnny to evaluate his behavior is also crucial. As children learn the purpose of the social-problem-solving meetings and realize that no one will be blamed or punished, they begin to acknowledge and evaluate their behavior and then look for better solutions.

A fourth grade teacher recently told me of a situation in which she used a social-problem-solving meeting. It seems that while in the library two of the boys in her class had gotten into a fight over who would check out a book about a favorite football player. The teacher was glad these boys had found a book of interest since they were not usually

67

enthusiastic about reading, but of course, she was concerned about their behavior. Later in the day, after the two boys had calmed down, she suggested a class meeting to talk over what had happened. When Tim, the boy who had just been reprimanded by the librarian, was asked what he had done, he responded by saying, "Jimmy pushed me." The teacher explained that she had not asked what someone else had done but rather what he had done which had gotten him into trouble. Finally he indicated that he had pushed Jimmy but only after Jimmy had grabbed his book. When Jimmy was confronted with what behavior had gotten him into trouble, he responded by saying that he had not started it, that he had seen the book first, therefore it was rightfully his and that it was all Tim's fault. The teacher pointed out that she was not trying to find who was at fault but just wanted to know what he had done. After some hesitation, Jimmy stated that he had seen the book, wanted it very badly, had grabbed it away from Tim and then the fight began. The teacher's next step was to get the boys to evaluate their behavior. She asked each one how their behavior had helped them. Eventually they indicated that it had not helped them, since neither had gotten to check out the book and both had been isolated from the group for their behavior and had missed an interesting filmstrip. The teacher then asked how the problem could have been solved more effectively. At this point many students raised their hands wanting to present ideas. After many suggestions were presented, the boys were asked which ideas they thought would work best for them. They concluded that they could have shared the book or they could have asked the librarian if there was another equally interesting book. At this point one of the class members suggested that perhaps the librarian still had the book and might allow them to implement this solution if they told her of their plan. The boys agreed to approach the librarian after school, explain the solution and see if the plan could be implemented. Even if the book was no longer available they both agreed that in the future if something similar happened they would implement their plan.

Although this matter was settled for the time being, this does not mean that future conflicts will always be averted even between the same two boys. It takes time for children to learn that problems can be solved in a new way. Sometimes children need the help of the group and eventually where there is conflict, students themselves may introduce the problem to the group rather than fight or engage in other

irresponsible behavior. Teachers should realize that
some problems are not easily resolved or may have no
apparent solution. Johnny continues to be a bully even
after his behavior has been discussed, or a child's
home life is torn apart by divorce and there is nothing
that can be done. Even in instances like these, the
discussion can be beneficial. Students learn that
sharing difficult problems with others helps them face
life realistically. They learn that everyone has
strengths and weaknesses and that when problems are
discussed, they become less frightening and more
tolerable.

Some Suggestions for Conducting
Classroom Meetings

Glasser makes a number of suggestions concerning
the mechanics of class meetings based upon his experience with these meetings in schools. Glasser is to be
admired because he has not just developed these ideas
and advocated their implementation. Instead, he
worked in schools conducting classroom meetings to see
if these meetings could be successfully implemented.
From these experiences, Glasser offers the following
suggestions concerning how class meetings can be
effectively utilized.

1. The meetings must take place in a circle.
    This allows everyone to be a part of the
    group. Any other seating arrangement will
    lessen the effectiveness of the discussion.

2. The teacher may need to arrange students in
    the circle so that disruptions will be mini-
    mized. It is helpful if the teacher takes a
    different seat in the circle each day. This
    allows the teacher to sit by different stu-
    dents in order to encourage those who do not
    talk or to inhibit misbehavior by those who
    might be disruptive.

3. The teacher or any class member can introduce
    subjects for discussion in open-ended and
    social-behavioral class meetings. The teacher
    may need to decide whether a subject is appro-
    priate or guide the discussion so that the
    meeting has the proper emphasis.

4. Meetings for the purpose of discussing disci-
    plinary problems should not concentrate on
    the same child and the same problems each day.

Glasser believes that disciplinary meetings are not the best way to get students involved with each other in a positive way. This kind of involvement is more likely to occur in open-ended or educational-diagnostic meetings which are interesting and provoke enthusiastic discussion. The open-ended class meeting should be used most often even when discipline problems are prevalent. If the class suggests that a student's problem behavior be discussed over and over in the meetings, the teacher may need to indicate that since the student has not changed, something else should be discussed and that when this student's behavior improves his case can again be brought up.

5. The length of class meetings depends upon the age of the students. Young children may not be able to sustain attention much beyond 15 or 20 minutes, whereas older students can be actively involved for a whole period. The meetings should be perceived as important enough to be held regularly. Glasser suggests daily meetings held at regular times. If this is not possible, at least one meeting each week is essential for the program to be effective.

6. If students talk about personal problems related to their home life the teacher will need to decide whether to redirect the discussion. Teachers should remember that home related problems are relevant to students' lives and may not provoke adult-like anxieties in children; therefore, their discussion can be beneficial.

7. Teachers should be nonjudgmental in class meetings. They should not tell students they are wrong or communicate criticism of their comments. When the teacher is nonjudgmental, students usually begin to play a judgmental role. For instance, if Tommy says he is going to run away from school another student may respond by saying, "You shouldn't do that." The teacher should encourage an interaction between students as they think about different ways to solve problems. If students provide inaccurate information about subject matter during group discussions, teachers can review the subject later during class time to correct

misunderstandings, but this should not be done during class meetings. Remember, teachers need to refrain from being judgmental in class meetings while allowing students the right to make judgments.

8. When first initiating class meetings, the teacher will need to keep the discussion going. As students get more involved and learn more about free discussion, they will improve in their ability to maintain the discussion.

Dealing with Discipline*

The reality orientation makes a distinction between discipline and punishment. Discipline exists when an individual abides by reasonable rules and regulations for the sake of self and others. In doing this the individual is making life better for himself and for those with whom he associates. On the other hand, punishment occurs when rules are enforced by threatening pain or by administering pain. In this instance, if an individual obeys rules it is to avoid something negative. The reality approach emphasizes discipline rather than punishment. Punishment leads to a devaluation of a person's sense of love and worth. Schools should be places where students want to abide by rules because they realize that doing so is best for them and others. Students can learn to respect themselves and others and abide by reasonable rules and regulations in schools which are characterized by the following elements:

1. The school is perceived by students as a good place. This is done by instituting some of the changes which have already been mentioned, i.e., class meetings to increase involvement and thinking, eliminating failure, deemphasizing the importance of right answers and removing the threat of punishment. Good schools are friendly places where teachers are concerned about students and show this concern through involvement. When the changes Glasser recommends are instituted, students will begin to view school in a more positive manner.

---

*Parts of this discussion are based upon the content of the films listed at the end of this chapter.

2. The students should take part in making the
   rules. If students help determine what rules
   are important, they are more likely to agree
   with and abide by the rules. This matter of
   agreement is important. If students agree
   that the class rules are good rules and are
   needed to make the school a better place, then
   discipline can exist.

3. Students should know the rules. Teachers need
   to review rules occasionally with students to
   make sure everyone is informed. Avoid having
   mystery rules--that is, rules that no one
   knows about until they are enforced.

4. Students should be aware of the consequences
   of rule violation. What consequences should
   occur when rules are violated will be discussed in the following section.

Making Schools a Better Place
Through Involvement

Although class meetings are the keystone of involvement, teachers must be aware of other ways to show
their genuine concern for students. One sixth grade
teacher was able to initiate individual conferences
with students for the purpose of getting to know them
better. Through these conferences she was able to
determine more about each student's interests and exhibit her concern for them in a personal way. In
another instance, an elementary school librarian, who
frequently had trouble with one of the sixth grade
girls during library period, asked the girl to stay for
a moment after class. The girl, not knowing of the
reality orientation, was sure she was going to be punished. The librarian, realizing that the girl would
not change until involvement was established, asked the
girl if she would come by the library before school
each morning for the next week just to say "hello."
Even though this was a very unusual request, the girl
agreed. Each morning the librarian showed an interest
in the girl during their brief conversation. After
several days they were able to chat for a few minutes.
The involvement which developed later made it possible
for the librarian to work with the girl in order to get
a commitment for improved behavior.

These examples indicate that there are many ways
to show concern through involvement. Teachers must
actively seek opportunities to communicate their

concern. Don't make the mistake of believing that this
is inappropriate. Actually, it is essential if good
discipline is to exist. If you remember, students who
are behaving in irresponsible ways are failing to satisfy their needs for love and worth. You can help them
satisfy these needs through involvement. If you are
successful, they begin to feel better about themselves,
they like you better and are more willing to cooperate.

After Involvement: What Next?

As students learn that school is a good place and
that teachers are concerned about them, discipline becomes easier. Under these conditions, what steps
should be taken if students violate rules? If you
recall, Glasser believes that the consequences of rule
violation should be clear.

Focus on Behavior. If a student violates a rule
the teacher should ask the student, "What did you do?",
"What are you doing?" or "What's happening?" The focus
is on behavior and accepting responsibility for behavior. Children may have difficulty discussing their
behavior. When asked what they are doing, they often
reply "Nothing" or "He did it" or "It was their fault."
All of these responses serve to avoid the question.
The teacher must continue to ask "What did you do?"
If students cannot accept responsibility for their
behavior, it is unlikely they will change. It will be
easier for students to admit their behavior to you and
to themselves if they have been told that the consequences of rule violation do not involve punishment.
Remember, reality therapy does not punish. Its focus
is on helping people change their behavior and accepting no excuses for being irresponsible. Nor does the
reality orientation ask, "Why did you behave that
way?" This would only direct attention away from what
the individual is doing and make it more difficult to
teach responsibility for one's own behavior. Without
the threat of punishment, children usually learn to
admit their behavior. They learn to say, "Well, I hit
him" or "I threw the paper out the window." Admitting
behavior is crucial since the next step cannot be
successful until students accept responsibility for
their behavior.

Evaluating Behavior. After the student has owned
his behavior, he must then evaluate it. The teacher
can help by asking, "Did your behavior help you or the
other students in the class?" Frequently students will
say "No." Sometimes they will respond with answers

like "It sure made me feel better to hit him" or "Yes, because he deserved it." In these cases the teacher must also ask whether the behavior was beneficial to the other student. This teaches students that they have some responsibility for the welfare of others. When involvement is strong and students are aware of the reality orientation they usually admit that their behavior was not helpful. This evaluation is important and leads to the next step of the reality approach.

Making a Plan. Once students have evaluated their behavior, then it is necessary to help them plan a new course of action. "What can you do which will help you abide by the rules?" At first students may not understand this question. They do not know what making a plan means. They may respond with "I don't know what to do" or give a negative response indicating what they will not do, such as "I will not misbehave again." The teacher must help students understand what is meant by making a plan and stating it in a positive way. Even small plans are acceptable and may actually be best if students have trouble carrying out long-term plans. If students cannot think of a plan or if they suggest an unrealistic plan, the teacher may need to offer suggestions. "Do you think you could . . ." is sometimes used to suggest a plan. Some examples are: "Do you think you could obey the rule if I moved you away from George?" "Do you think you could cooperate and finish the project if you worked with another student rather than alone?" "Do you think you could bring your own gym equipment and dress out tomorrow?"

Usually plans relate specifically to correcting an inappropriate response but this need not always be the case. At times children who exhibit problem behavior need the experience of being able to carry out a plan just for the feeling of satisfaction and accomplishment. In one such case, the teacher asked a student if he would be willing to help a younger child learn to kick a football. The teacher, knowing that the misbehaving student was good at sports, was trying to help him gain a sense of worth through accomplishment. Later, perhaps the child could carry out other plans relating more directly to classroom behavior.

The reality orientation believes that making a plan to behave in responsible ways is important. This allows students to take the initiative for improving and to feel successful and worthwhile when the plan is carried out.

Sealing the Agreement. After a plan has been agreed upon, usually the teacher asks the student to carry it out. This may be a verbal agreement culminating in a hand shake or a nod, or a written agreement signed by the student. Some teachers have even had students tape record their agreements to carry out their plans. Regardless of how it is done, this step is important because it emphasizes the student's responsibility to carry through on the plan. Frequently it will be obvious to the teacher when a student fulfills or fails to fulfill a plan. When it is not obvious, students need to know that the teacher will check back with them or that they are to report to the teacher on the progress they are making. At times, two students may need to work together with the teacher in devising a plan since the problem involves both students.

Responding to misbehavior by asking "What are you doing?", "How is it helping you?" and "Can you make a plan?" cannot always be carried out immediately. Sometimes students need to calm down before they can think rationally and at other times the teacher must give immediate attention to other matters. In these instances, the teacher can indicate to the student that the problem will be discussed at a later time.

No Punishment and No Excuses. If a problem cannot be dealt with immediately, the teacher can send the student to a designated quiet area. This removes the student from the activities of the class but is not perceived as punishment. Its purpose is to help the student calm down so that a plan can be developed; not to hurt the student or inflict pain through the removal of positive experiences. As soon as the student is willing to develop a plan to behave appropriately, then he can return to the regular activities of the class. Students should know that this is the way the quiet area time is used and that being sent to this area will not be followed by punishment or threats of punishment. Should the student complain that he is being punished, the teacher should explain the purpose of the quiet area and indicate that working out and agreeing to a realistic plan is all that is needed to return to class. The quiet area may be a place within the classroom or a place outside the class. If the administration and the faculty are working together to implement a reality approach, a schoolwide quiet area can be used. When a student is sent to this area, a counselor or teacher can be available to assist the student in focusing on and evaluating behavior and then making a plan. Remember, the class should be a good place so that students will eventually want to go back to their regular program and be with their friends.

Positive results from using a reality approach may be fairly immediate or may take some time. Students who lack involvement and feel they have nothing to gain by being in school are hard to reach. Even when teachers are doing their best to make the school a good place, some students will continue to be behavioral problems. They will make and break plans. It is not easy for a person who has behaved irresponsibly for many years to all of a sudden behave in a responsible way. This takes time and the teacher should be willing to continue to work with students even though they break agreements. Teachers must give students another chance to develop and carry out new plans. In this respect, the reality orientation never gives up. Nor does this approach accept excuses. When students who fail to carry out plans want to explain away their failure, the teacher must focus on the students' behavior and the development of another plan. In one instance, a high school girl had been helped to develop ten plans, each of which she had failed to carry through. On the eleventh occasion she asked the counselor when they were going to give up. She was told that they would not give up. The girl then broke down and cried, stating that no one had ever been concerned about her before. She finally made a plan and was able to follow it through. Although this was just one small step toward helping her gain love and worth, it was a step in the right direction.

Some Things to Remember. The reality orientation applied to school settings involves the following:

1. The school must be a good place. Glasser believes that showing concern through involvement, making the curriculum more relevant, emphasizing thinking rather than the memorization of facts, changing the grading system so that no one is labeled a failure, having classroom meetings, and grouping by age, not ability, are steps which will help achieve this objective.

2. Students must take part in the development of classroom rules. There should be no mystery rules. School rules should be reviewed periodically to make sure students know them.

3. The consequences of rule violation should be clear. This means that students should be aware of the reality orientation to problem solving.

4. When students break rules they are asked to focus on their behavior and what they are doing.

5. After students have indicated what they are doing, they are asked to evaluate this behavior. Was their behavior helpful to them or others in the classroom? If involvement is strong and the reality orientation is known, students can realistically evaluate their behavior.

6. After students have evaluated their behavior they are asked to make a plan which will lead to improvement. If students are unable to do so, the teacher can suggest a plan.

7. When a plan is worked out, the student is asked to agree to the plan. This is important because it emphasizes the student's responsibility to fulfill the plan.

8. If students fail to carry out plans they are not punished. Instead, they are given a chance to develop another plan and to try again. No excuses are accepted for failure, since this would tend to relieve students of their responsibility for behavior.

Summary

Reality therapy was developed by Dr. William Glasser, a psychiatrist who rebelled against the traditional psychoanalytic approach to therapy. The reality therapist expresses concern for patients through involvement, stresses the individual's personal responsibility for behavior, helps patients evaluate their behavior and institute plans to change. If the patient fails to carry out a plan, the therapist does not punish or accept excuses. To do so would only reinforce a sense of failure which the patient already perceives due to an inability to satisfy the needs of love and worth. Instead, the therapist continues to encourage the patient to carry out plans and be responsible.

After successfully implementing the reality approach in a school for delinquent girls and a mental hospital, Glasser turned his attention to the problems of schools. He indicated that schools engage in practices (e.g., emphasizing memorization rather than thinking, labeling students as failures, teaching irrelevant subject matter), which alienate students and oftentimes reinforce a failure identity. To make constructive changes, school must be made more relevant to students' interests and needs. Students should take part in developing the rules and teachers should attempt to show a genuine concern for students through involvement. One way to increase involvement is through the use of classroom meetings where students' ideas and opinions about a wide range of subjects are elicited. This not only communicates to students that teachers are interested and willing to listen, it also communicates to them that their interests and ideas are important. These and other changes, such as making the curriculum more relevant, emphasizing thinking rather than memorization, and changing the traditional grading system, will help make the school a better place.

Discipline exists when the students abide by school rules for the sake of self and others. When the school is a good place and the students have had a part in developing the rules, they are more likely to abide by the rules. In every school, however, rules will be broken. When this happens, students are helped to focus on their behavior and asked to evaluate it in terms of whether it helped them and their classmates. If the answer is "No" students then make a plan to change. If students are successful in implementing their plans, they have become more responsible. If they are unsuccessful the teacher should not punish or accept excuses. Rather, the teacher must continue to help students develop and carry out realistic plans. It is through responsible behavior that students learn to properly satisfy their needs for love and worth and to develop success identities.

CASE EXAMPLE 3-1

Gang, M. J., Cates, J. T., Poppen, W. and Thompson, G. "Classroom Discipline Problems and Reality Therapy: Research Support." Elementary School Guidance and Counseling, 1976, 11, 131-137.

This study examines the effect of reality therapy techniques on the incidence of desirable and undesirable behavior in a classroom setting. A fourth and fifth grade teacher were each asked to select three students who they considered to be behavioral problems and with whom they would like to establish a closer working relationship. The six children chosen as target students were all males.

During the first phase of the study (baseline) trained observers recorded the number of desirable and undesirable behaviors exhibited by the six target students. The teachers were then trained to use the following four techniques of reality therapy in dealing with the desirable and undesirable behavior of these students: (1) They were trained to become more involved with the students by talking briefly to each of them about either academic or nonacademic subjects three times during a class period. (2) The teachers were instructed to ask "What are you doing?" when the students were engaged in both desirable and undesirable behavior. (3) The teachers were trained to help students evaluate their behavior by asking, "Is what you are doing helpful to you or the class?" (4) When a student evaluated his behavior positively, the teacher was instructed to praise the student or help him develop a plan to continue the desirable response. When a student indicated that his behavior was not helpful, the teacher was instructed to help the student develop a plan to improve and then make a commitment to the plan.

After training, the teachers implemented the reality oriented procedures in two phases: (1) an initial involvement period in which the teachers talked briefly with the students at least three times during a class period, (2) a varied intervention period in which the teachers responded by using the reality therapy techniques for a specified number of days when students engaged in undesirable behavior, then when students engaged in desirable behavior, and, finally, when students engaged in both desirable and undesirable behavior. At the end of this intervention period, trained observers continued to monitor student behavior to determine if any changes in behavior which occurred during intervention would be maintained.

During the initial involvement period when the teachers began taking a special interest in the target students, undesirable behavior decreased 17 percent when compared with baseline data and desirable behavior increased 69 percent. For the entire intervention period (i.e., when the teachers used reality therapy techniques to respond to undesirable behavior, then to desirable behavior and finally to both desirable and undesirable behavior), it was found that desirable behavior increased 222 percent over baseline and undesirable behavior decreased 56 percent. The teachers' reality oriented responses to desirable behavior produced the most improvement in student behavior, although the other responses also produced significant improvement. During the two-week follow-up period, the improvements in behavior made by the target students continued to be exhibited.

Marandola, P. and Imber, S. "Glasser's Classroom Meeting: A Humanistic Approach to Behavior Change with Pre-adolescent Inner-City Learning Disabled Children." Journal of Learning Disabilities, 1979, 12, 383-387.

There has been a great deal of interest in Glasser's concept of classroom meetings. This study attempted to evaluate the effectiveness of class meetings on the argumentative behavior of a class of inner-city learning disabled children. Ten boys between the ages of eleven and twelve served as subjects in this experiment. The achievement level of all these students was at least two years below grade level and many exhibited behavioral characteristics, e.g., tantrums, aggression, short attention span, hyperactivity, which presented problems in the classroom. One of the main concerns of the teacher was the frequency of verbal arguments and physical confrontations among students. Prior to introducing classroom meetings, the students were observed for fourteen days (baseline period) and the occurrence of verbal arguments and physical confrontations was recorded. The teacher then introduced classroom meetings, having meetings daily for an eight-day period. The meetings were of the open-ended and problem-solving type and frequently addressed questions related to argumentative behavior such as "What can we do in the classroom to help students get along?" or "What happens when people don't get along with one another?" The researchers hoped the students would be able to reflect on the issue of cooperation and conflict in interpersonal relationships. A record of verbal arguments and physical confrontations was also recorded during this intervention period.

An analysis of the results indicated that arguments and physical confrontations decreased significantly during the intervention period. Verbal arguments between two students were reduced from an average of 3.79 per day during the fourteen-day baseline period to an average of 0.25 per day during the eight intervention days. Arguments involving more than two students decreased from an average of 1.21 per day to an average of 0.38 per day. Physical confrontations were also drastically reduced from a baseline rate of 0.38 per day to an intervention rate of 0.13 per day--or a reduction of 67 percent. The researchers conclude from this study that "strong support has been provided regarding the methodology of classroom meetings and its role in behavior change."

CASE EXAMPLE 3-3

Margolis, H., Muhlfelder, C., and Brannigan, G. "Reality Therapy and Underachievement: A Case Study." Education, 1977, 98(2), 153-155.

This study examines the effect of a reality orientation on Mark, a 15-year-old high school student with a history of poor academic performance and aggressive behavior. Mark was perceived by his peers as someone who prided himself in creating class disturbances and causing problems for the teacher. He would frequently shout out in class, initiate fights and make obscene gestures.

Mark spent one period each day in a special education mathematics class. Reality oriented strategies were implemented with Mark in this class in an attempt to improve academic performance and decrease disruptive behavior. A university practicum student assigned to this class was given the responsibility of establishing a facilitative relationship with Mark. The practicum student's reality orientation was exhibited by the following characteristics:

1. Establishing involvement with Mark by talking to him, especially about things he found interesting such as auto mechanics, weight-lifting, and the Air Force.

2. Accepting and respecting Mark as a person of importance.

3. Modeling responsible behavior so that Mark could see that meeting responsible standards, such as concern for others and attention to detail, was important.

4. Assisting Mark in setting his own goals and standards.

5. Helping Mark see what he would have to do if he was to accomplish these goals.

6. Accepting no excuse for failing to accomplish academic and behavioral goals.

7. Refraining from using punishment when Mark's behavior was disruptive or his work incomplete.

8. Communicating to Mark that he was capable of meeting his standards and goals.

9. Focusing attention on present behavior rather than past experience.

Using these strategies, test results indicated that Mark made substantial progress in mathematics. Furthermore, the researcher reported that Mark engaged in more appropriate behavior, eliminated his disruptive mannerisms, and began to interact with others in a more responsible way.

INVOLVEMENT EXERCISES

1. What are the major reasons for having class meetings?

2. Suggest three topics for an open-ended class meeting which you believe would be appropriate for your class or a class you might teach. (For ideas other than your own, chapter 12 in Glasser's book <u>Schools</u> <u>Without</u> <u>Failure</u> offers some excellent suggestions.)

3. Review the educational materials which you use or will use in your class and suggest four topics which would be appropriate for an educational-diagnostic class meeting.

4. Indicate when you would use a social-problem-solving meeting and suggest three problems which would be appropriate for discussion in these meetings.

5. How can schools be made "good" places for students to learn?

6. Other than through the use of class meetings, how can you exhibit involvement and a sense of concern for your students?

7. John, a sixth grader in your class, is very disruptive and hard to manage. You have tried punitive tactics but they have not worked. You have just read about the importance of involvement. What can you do to communicate an interest and concern for John in your attempt to become involved?

8. Two of your students, Robbie and Jim, are fighting on the playground. You have shown concern and involvement for these students and have used the reality approach to discipline with your class. Using this approach, how would you confront Robbie and Jim (i.e., what would you say to them), and ideally how might they respond?

9. Think of some responses which students might give when you ask them, "What are you doing?" which allow them to avoid focusing on their own behavior. How would you respond to these kinds of comments?

0. Your principal has heard about your reality approach to discipline. You realize she believes in using a more punitive approach. One afternoon she asks you about reality therapy and what you think you are accomplishing. How would you respond?

1. Tim is the class clown. Although he is a good-natured child, he is always disrupting your fifth grade class by interrupting while others are talking, seeking attention by doing outlandish things, and distracting other students. Suggest some plans that Tim might agree to implement, which if carried out would help him become more responsible.

12. Roberta has made and broken many plans. She has just told you that she'll probably never be able to carry out a plan. As her teacher, how would you respond?

13. You are going to initiate the reality approach to discipline in your classroom. First you must explain the approach and specify how misbehavior will be handled. Outline what you would say to your students.

REFERENCES

Glasser, W. The identity society. New York: Harper and Row, 1961.

Glasser, W. Mental health or mental illness? New York: Harper and Row, 1961.

Glasser, W. Reality therapy. New York: Harper and Row Publishers, 1965.

Glasser, W. "Reality therapy, a realistic approach to the young offender." Journal of Crime and Delinquency, 1964, 135-44.

Glasser, W. Schools without failure. New York: Harper and Row Publishers, 1969.

Glasser, W., and Zunin, L. "Reality therapy." In Raymond Corsini (Ed.), Current psychotherapies. Itasca, Ill.: F. E. Peacock Publishers, 1973, pp. 287-315.

Films

The following films present aspects of the reality orientation:

Reality Therapy in High School

Why Class Meetings?

Dealing with Discipline Problems

Glasser on Discipline

CHAPTER 4

THE HUMANISTIC APPROACH TO
CLASSROOM MANAGEMENT

In an attempt to help students understand the humanistic approach to classroom management, this chapter will first present the work of Carl Rogers. A discussion of Rogers' ideas will serve to introduce the humanistic viewpoint and provide the groundwork for a discussion of the classroom management orientation of Dr. Thomas Gordon. Gordon presents his ideas concerning how teachers can be effective classroom managers in his book Teacher Effectiveness Training. Gordon drew upon the work of other humanists like Carl Rogers as he formulated his ideas about helping relationships. Prior to his interest in teaching, Gordon had focused his attention on childrearing. His book Parent Effectiveness Training, first published in 1970, had sold over 500,000 copies by 1974. The popularity of this book is due partly to the practical help it provides parents in communicating and relating to children. Many parents were in need of guidance and ready to accept a book which offered concrete suggestions on how to open channels of communication, deal with conflict and resolve problems. Teacher Effectiveness Training is based upon the same ideas suggested for parents but with certain modifications for the special problems found in school situations.

Carl Rogers and His Influence

Carl Rogers has been a leading spokesman for the humanistic movement for many years. Although he is trained as a clinical psychologist and became known in the 1940's for his work in psychotherapy, today his influence has been felt in many sectors of life, including education. Rogers, like Glasser, believed that the traditional psychoanalytic approach to therapy was often ineffective. He concluded that examining a patient's past history, analyzing unconscious processes and providing insight into the origins of a problem were not conducive to bringing about constructive change. In 1951 Rogers published his theory of personality and psychotherapy in the book Client-Centered Therapy: Its Current Practice, Implications, and Theory.

Rogers' Theory of Personality

The Actualizing Tendency. According to Rogers,
all individuals have an innate tendency to develop in
positive ways. This growth potential is referred to as
the actualizing tendency and it is nurtured in certain
kinds of environments. Rogers refers to this positive
growth when he states:

> I find it significant that when individuals
> are prized as persons, the values they select
> do not run the full gamut of possibilities. I
> do not find, in such a climate of freedom, that
> one person comes to value fraud and murder and
> thievery, while another values a life of self-
> sacrifice, and another values only money.
> Instead there seems to be a deep and underlying
> thread of commonality. I believe that when the
> human being is inwardly free to choose whatever
> he deeply values he tends to value those objects,
> experiences, and goals which make for his own
> survival growth, and development, and for the
> survival and development of others. I hypothe-
> size that it is characteristic of the human
> organism to prefer such actualizing and social-
> ized goals when he is exposed to a growth
> promoting climate (1964, p. 166).

Rogers' belief in the individual's worth and goodness
and in the tendency of the individual to strive toward
self-actualization characterizes not only his approach
but the whole thrust of the humanistic movement.

Evaluating Experience. Rogers believes that individuals evaluate their experience in light of the
actualizing tendency. That is, does the experience
promote growth toward self-actualization. Rogers
refers to this valuing process as the organismic valuing process. When experiences (including feelings,
thoughts, and behavior) are consistent with the positive, forward thrust of the actualizing tendency, they
are satisfying and evaluated positively. When experiences are inconsistent with the thrust of the actualizing tendency, they are unsatisfying and evaluated
negatively. The organismic valuing process, then,
allows the individual to assess experience in light of
the actualizing tendency. Rogers concludes that this
approach to valuing is present even in the infant, as
can be seen, for instance, when food and security are
positively valued and hunger and pain are negatively
valued. The valuing process is a flexible process with

hange occurring frequently. The hungry infant values
ood positively but a few minutes later after consuming
ood, evaluates it negatively by turning away and spit-
ing it out. Infants do not need to be told to make
hese evaluations; rather, their origin is centered
within themselves.

Man's Worth and Goodness. It is important to
gain point out that Rogers believes in the individu-
l's worth and goodness. Human beings are innately
ositive, forward-moving and constructive. When indi-
iduals are free to choose their values, they tend to
alue experiences which lead to personal growth and
development as well as the growth and development of
thers. If individuals are free from environmental
ressures, they are capable of making correct decisions
oncerning what is best for them and for mankind.
ogers' experiences in therapy have reinforced this
elief because it is in the therapeutic environment
hat he has seen clients grow and develop in positive
ways. Certainly individuals do not always exhibit
ositive traits but from the humanistic viewpoint,
hortcoming, e.g., greed, jealousy, etc., stem from
nvironmental factors, not innate characteristics.

When Things Go Wrong

Unhealthy Environments. Although the actualizing
tendency's thrust toward self-actualization is innate,
t can be thrown off course when an individual is exposed to an unhealthy environment. Rogers believes
hat as children mature, a concept of self develops.
When this occurs, individuals have an idea of who
hey are and can evaluate their experience in light of
his self-perception. Those experiences which are
onsistent with the self are positively valued; those
experiences which are inconsistent with the self are
negatively valued. This makes the development of the
self-concept a very important aspect of an individual's
makeup. The actualizing tendency's thrust toward self-
actualization can be thwarted when a child is pressured
by parents and others to value objects and beliefs
which are inconsistent with the child's own organismic
valuing process and experience. This could result in
a self-concept which is inconsistent with experience.

Baron, Byrne and Kantowitz (1977) give an example
of how this could happen. The parents of a three-year-
old boy have just had a new baby. The three-year-old
is upset because now he is no longer the center of
attention but must watch while others bestow affection

89

upon the infant. The boy now feels unloved, rejected and hostile. One day the mother finds the boy venting his hostility toward the baby by pinching her arm. At this point the mother must make a decision concerning how to respond to her son. Will she make a response which will nurture the good qualities within the boy or will she respond in a way which will tend to increase hostility and alienation?

Baron, Byrne and Kantowitz explain that it would not be unusual for a parent to punish and reject the child because of his hostility. "I don't know what got into you. You're not my little boy if you act like that. You know you love baby sister. Give her a kiss and say you're sorry" (p. 305). In this instance the mother has communicated that her love is conditional and is based upon her son's love for his sister. The problem for the boy is apparent. He knows that he does not feel positive toward baby sister and would rather pinch her than kiss her. However, the need for love from his mother is vitally important, so much so that he may be forced to convince himself and his mother that he really does love sister even though many of his later inner experiences and feelings are inconsistent with this belief. In this situation, the mother's conditional love has forced the boy to hide his true feelings and to introject a value (I must always love sister) which is not his own. These two consequences are not conducive to positive psychological growth.

Many times as children grow up, they are pressured to deny aspects of their experiences or lose the love of a parent. If this happens, parents are placing conditions of worth on their children since they are willing to love only if their children meet certain conditions. The following statements will serve as examples of how parental injunctions can place children in a conflict between their experience (which may be natural) and the loss of parental love, especially when these injunctions are associated, implicitly or explicitly, with behavior on the part of the parent which threatens loss of love.

* "Don't you ever talk back to your daddy again. You're not to disagree with your daddy." (The implication here is that the child should never have or express feeling when there is disagreement.)

* "Don't you ever let me find out you've skipped school again. You'll like school and that's an order." (The implication here is that the child should always have positive feelings toward school.)

* Don't you ever treat your playmates like that again. They're your guests and it's an insult to me when you won't play with them." (The implication here is that children should always enjoy playing with their playmates regardless of circumstances.)

* "If I ever catch you smoking pot, that will be the end. You can just get out." (The implication here is that to satisfy this curiosity will result in immediate loss of love.)

Incongruence. Statements like those mentioned above coupled with threatened loss of love help children incorporate into their self-concept ideas which are narrow and rigid and may run counter to inner experiencing. When an individual is no longer acting in a way which honestly reflects inner experiencing, that individual is said to be incongruent. Individuals who are incongruent no longer use the organismic valuing process in evaluating experience. Instead, they have introjected the values of others and use these values in the valuing process. Rogers believes that most adults use the introjected values of others in assessing experience. They place the same conditions of worth on themselves that were previously placed upon them by parents and significant others. When this happens experiences which are congruent with one's conditions of worth are accurately perceived whereas experiences which are incongruent with one's conditions of worth are denied or distorted.

Defense Mechanisms. The utilization of denial and distortion is significant. These defense mechanisms prevent individuals from gaining an awareness of experiences which would be beneficial for constructive growth and development. Furthermore, if a feeling or experience is repressed through denial or distortion it may build up in the form of tension and be expressed later in such a strong way that it causes harm to a relationship. When an incongruent experience begins to surface to a conscious level of awareness rather than being completely denied or sufficiently distorted, the individual becomes anxious. Rogers believes that everyone experiences some incongruence and anxiety; it is

only when incongruence is severe or frequent that maladjustment occurs.

The Need for Unconditional
Positive Regard

What Children Need. As the self develops the
individual experiences a need for positive regard.
Rogers feels that this need is universal although he is
uncertain whether its origin is innate or learned.
Children need to feel accepted, loved, and prized. As
we have seen, parents frequently exhibit this attitude
toward children when they engage in desirable behavior.
When their children's behavior, attitude, etc. is in
some way undesirable, as was the case when the boy
pinched his baby sister, conditions are placed on the
child's worth. Love is made contingent on the child's
desirable behavior. As parents exhibit love and
acceptance toward children for certain behaviors, the
children themselves develop a need for positive self-
regard. That is, the children begin to view themselves in positive ways only when they incorporate the
standards of their parents into their self-structure.
Behaviors which parents view in positive ways are
introjected by their children, making it mandatory that
their children adhere to these standards of behavior if
they are to view themselves positively. We have already seen how repeated experiences with conditions of
worth can have a detrimental effect on development by
alienating the individual from his own organismic
valuing process and experience. What the child needs
is not a conditional kind of positive regard, but an
unconditional positive regard. This regard communicates acceptance and love for the child as a person in
spite of shortcomings and faults. Rogers contends that
if unconditional positive regard always existed children would be more congruent (in touch with and guided
by their organismic valuing process) and, therefore,
more psychologically healthy. Even though communicating unconditional positive regard may be difficult,
it is an essential ingredient for the healthy development of the individual.

Childrearing. Although it may appear that Rogers
would allow children to do whatever they please, this
is not the case. He believes in a democratic approach
to childrearing in which children are prized and their
feelings accepted even though some behaviors cannot be
permitted. Such an approach could theoretically be
achieved if the parent genuinely expressed the following kind of attitude when unacceptable behavior occurs:

"I can understand how satisfying it feels to
you to hit your baby brother (or to defecate
when and where your please or to destroy things)
and I love you and am quite willing for you to
have those feelings. But I am quite willing
for me to have my feelings, too, and I feel
very distressed, . . . and so I do not let you
hit him. Both your feelings and my feelings
are important, and each of us can freely have
his own" (1959, p. 225).

What, then, should the parent do when the child
misbehaves? Returning to the example of the boy who
pinched his baby sister, what should the mother have
done? Certainly she cannot allow the boy to continue
to pinch his sister. First, the mother can recognize
the child's feelings and accept these feelings. A
comment such as "Sometimes you do get mad at sister
and want to hurt her" communicates some understanding
of the child's inner experience. The parent does not
have to like what the child has done but it is important to recognize the child's feelings and what is
going on inside him. Secondly, the mother should not
threaten loss of love. If she could see the world from
the viewpoint of her young son she could understand
that he already feels some threat and rejection from
those whose love he needs most. Thirdly, after recognizing the child's feelings and accepting them without
threatening loss of love, the mother can express her
genuine concern about the boy's behavior. "I'm upset
when I see you pinching baby sister. I'm afraid you'll
hurt her." This comment clearly communicates the
mother's feelings. Fourthly, the hostile behavior must
be prevented.

By responding in this way, the mother is communicating unconditional positive regard and is able to
retain her own identity by expressing the deep concern
she has about her son's behavior and the welfare of the
baby. She is, from a Rogerian viewpoint, creating the
type of relationship which will allow the growing child
to develop positive feelings about himself and his
relationship with others.

Some Important Definitions

* The actualizing tendency is an innate tendency to
  develop in positive ways. It is the source of
  basic goodness since those individuals who are in
  touch with their actualizing tendency are positive,
  constructive and forward-moving.

* Conditions of worth are conditions which an individual must satisfy to receive the conditional positive regard of others. Repeated experiences with conditions of worth lead to the introjection of these conditions into an individual's self-structure. When this happens, these conditions serve as the criterion for positive self-regard.

* Congruence exists when an individual's experience is consistent with the organismic valuing process and when the self-concept is free from conditions of worth. When this occurs, individuals can be guided by their actualizing tendency.

* Incongruence occurs when an individual is no longer utilizing the organismic valuing process to evaluate experiences. Instead, conditions of worth become more important in the valuing process.

* Unconditional positive regard is the acceptance, love and prizing of an individual without making this positive regard contingent on certain behaviors, thoughts or feelings.

* Experience is the term used to refer to everything which an individual can be aware of at any given time. This can include feelings, perceptions, thoughts and behaviors.

* Anxiety is the state of uneasiness which results when an individual's experience is, to some extent, perceived as inconsistent with the self-concept.

* The organismic valuing process is the process which allows an individual to value positively those experiences which are consistent with the actualizing tendency and to value negatively those experiences which are inconsistent with the actualizing tendency.

* Self-actualization is a term which relates to the fulfillment of one's potential. Fulfillment comes when individuals are true to the self (living in accordance with their actualizing tendency). This is a continuous process toward which one must constantly strive.

* The self or self-concept is a sense of oneself as being separate and distinct from other people and things.

Summarizing: Things to Remember

1. Advocates of the humanistic viewpoint see human beings as basically good.

2. When individuals exhibit negative qualities, these are the result of environmental conditions, not innate characteristics.

3. Rogers' theory contends that human beings are motivated by their actualizing tendency to seek experiences which promote growth and which lead to self-actualization.

4. When conditions of worth are placed upon an individual by parents and significant others, an individual's need for positive regard may become stronger than the need to follow the organismic valuing process.

5. When this happens, individuals introject the values of others and live in accordance with these values rather than following their organismic valuing process.

6. When values are introjected, the self-concept is based upon the dictates of others, and not on the ability of the organismic valuing process to determine what is best for the individual. This leads to a state of incongruence.

7. At times an individual's experience (behaviors, thoughts, feelings) is inconsistent with the individual's concept of self. This also is referred to as incongruence.

8. Incongruence may result in anxiety and is defended against by the utilization of defense mechanisms (denial and distortion).

9. Everyone is moderately incongruent at times; it is only when incongruence is frequent and severe that maladjustment occurs.

10. In order for individuals to develop their full potential they need to experience unconditional positive regard rather than conditions of worth. This would allow them to be open to all inner experiencing. Unconditional positive regard would reduce threat and anxiety

and eliminate the utilization of defense mechanisms.

11. Rogers further contends that individuals need to experience relationships with people who are genuine and who communicate empathic understanding. These conditions nurture the individual's innate goodness and produce those traits which characterize the fully functioning person. We will say more about this in the next section of this chapter.

Psychotherapy: Nurturing Man's Goodness

Since man has goodness which comes from within, it is necessary to provide an environment which is conducive to the nurturing and growth of this goodness. In client-centered therapy,* the name given to Rogers' approach to treatment, the type of environment created by the therapist is the most crucial factor affecting the success of the therapeutic process.

The client-centered therapist attempts to create a relationship which provides those ingredients necessary for positive growth and development. Rogers (1961) stressed the importance of the relationship when he stated: "If I can provide a certain type of relationship, the other person will discover within himself the capacity to use that relationship for growth and change, and personal development will occur" (p. 33).

What are the ingredients of such a relationship which a therapist must provide for positive change to take place? According to Rogers (1967), it is essential that:

1. The therapist experiences unconditional positive regard for the client and is successful in communicating this to the client.

2. The therapist experiences empathic understanding of the client's point of view and is successful in communicating this understanding to the client.

---

*In Rogers' more recent writings he has referred to his approach as a person-centered approach since his theory has been effectively applied in many different settings other than therapy.

3. The therapist is genuine or congruent in the relationship.

Unconditional Positive Regard

Unconditional positive regard involves a genuine caring for the client as an individual. It is unconditional in that the client's feelings and thoughts are accepted without judgment or evaluation by the therapist. The therapist does not place stipulations on his caring such as "I accept you if you change your attitude" but rather communicates "I accept you the way you are." Clients in this environment are free to have their own thoughts without fear of being rejected by the therapist. In this type of atmosphere the client is able to drop defenses, examine all types of feelings and choose those values which are positive. It should be noted that this type of acceptance does not mean that the therapist is approving of all the client's behavior. In client-centered therapy there is the acceptance of the client's right to have thoughts and feelings, but not necessarily approval of the client's actions.

Empathic Understanding

Empathic understanding is another important aspect of the therapeutic relationship. This understanding occurs when the therapist is able to perceive the world in the way the client perceives the world and in doing so shares the client's subjective experience. When the therapist can see and feel from the client's point of view without losing his own identity, then Rogers belives the client can begin to make constructive changes. Of course, this empathic understanding of the client must not only be felt but also communicated so that the client actually perceives that at least to some degree the therapist understands what it is like to be the client. The following interaction between client and therapist will illustrate empathic understanding.

Client: I just don't know which way to turn. Things are so confusing to me that I feel like giving up.

Therapist: The problem seems so great that it appears unsolvable and in desperation you feel you just can't go on.

Client: That's right. It hasn't always been this
             way. There used to be some hope, but now
             I just don't know . . .

Therapist: It sounds like you feel things are even
             worse than before and now you're not sure
             if there's any hope left.

Being Real or Genuine

Rogers stresses the importance of being genuine,
real and congruent in the therapeutic relationship.
This means that the therapist does not put up a false
front or pretend to be one way outwardly while inwardly
feeling very differently. This translates into a kind
of honesty. The therapist is true to himself in that
his inner and outer experiences match and he is honest
with the client by expressing openly appropriate feelings which occur in the relationship. For Rogers this
genuineness is necessary if the client is to make
gains in therapy.

The Goal of Client-Centered Therapy

The goal of the client-centered therapist is to
create a climate which is characterized by warmth,
acceptance and understanding so that clients can drop
their defenses and facades. In this kind of environment individuals can move toward a greater openness to
the experiencing which is going on inside them. Rogers
believes that when individuals are moving toward greater openness they are better able to get in touch with
their inner core of goodness and in doing so will begin
to value those things which enhance their own development and the development of others. What are the
values toward which the fully functioning individual
will move? Rogers (1969) sees the following value directions in his clients as they move toward maturity:

* They tend to move away from facades. Pretense,
  defensiveness, putting up a front, tend to be
  negatively valued.

* They tend to move away from "oughts." The com-
  pelling feeling of "I ought to do or be thus and
  so" is negatively valued.

* They tend to move away from meeting the expectations of others. Pleasing others as a goal in
  itself is negatively valued.

* Being real is positively valued. The client tends to move toward being himself, being his real feelings, being what he is.

* Self-direction is positively valued. The client discovers an increasing pride and confidence in making his own choices, guiding his own life.

* The client comes to value an openness to all of his inner and outer experience.

* One's self, one's own feelings come to be positively valued.

* Sensitivity to others and acceptance of others is positively valued.

* Deep relationships are positively valued (pp. 253-254).

These value directions are allowed to develop in a relationship where the therapist is genuine and communicates unconditional positive regard and empathic understanding. If we can be this certain about the ingredients of relationships which are necessary for nurturing goodness, should we not strive to provide such relationships for everyone? The humanist believes we must create such environments. Just as a gardener attempts to provide an environment which is conducive to the growth and maturity of his plants, the humanist strives to create environments for people which allow them to grow and mature in constructive ways.

Humanism and Education

Many humanists have written on the subect of education. In 1969 Carl Rogers expanded his influence to this area with the publication of the book Freedom to Learn. In this book Rogers deals with issues which are essential to humanistic education. His ideas on education stem directly from the philosophy underlying client-centered therapy. Basically, Rogers believes that students can be trusted to provide their own direction concerning what learnings are important for them. This can occur when the teacher creates an environment which is characterized by freedom and trust. Essentially, the teacher must be honest, acceptant, understanding and willing to let students explore those things which are meaningful to them. Such an approach seems very radical to those who advocate traditional methods, but Rogers contends that if just a few.

teachers would provide student-centered classrooms, education would be changed for the better in a relatively short time.

The Student-Centered Classroom. According to Rogers, the goal of education and the goal of psychotherapy are the same: the fully-functioning person. Education directed toward the memorization of facts is ineffective. It does not focus on the whole person since it ignores feelings and personal meaning. Learning which has personal meaning is significant because it is perceived as relevant. Many times this type of learning is acquired by doing; that is, by becoming involved with practical or real problems. Learning is also more meaningful when students participate in the development of their own objectives, plan and determine their own directions and formulate their own problems.

The environment most supportive of this kind of exploring and learning is one that is free from pressure, ridicule and threat. It is an environment characterized by acceptance and understanding of the students' fears, mistakes and feelings. This kind of environment reduces the students' resistance to change and makes it possible for them to be open to new experiences and learning.

Teaching in the student-centered classroom is much different than in the traditional classroom. Rogers believes that teaching as we traditionally know it is a vastly over-rated function. Since self-initiated and self-discovered learning is the only learning which significantly influences behavior, Rogers questions whether learning can be taught. From this viewpoint, the teacher should not be someone who imparts knowledge but a facilitator of learning in others. To be a facilitator the teacher must provide the conditions which lead to meaningful self-initiated learning. The conditions which allow individuals to explore new meanings in psychotherapy are the same conditions which are needed to facilitate learning in educational settings.

Realness and Genuineness. To be facilitators, teachers must be honest, open and willing to share their feelings with students. These teachers are in touch with themselves and are able to communicate their feelings regardless of whether they are positive or negative. If these teachers are angry they can say "I am angry" or if they are pleased they can say "I am pleased." This realness can be expressed without evaluating, blaming or judging others. Although this kind

100

of realness is difficult to communicate, it is essential to facilitate learning and should not be mistaken for a license to downgrade students. There is no place in education for harsh, uncaring teachers whose emotional problems cause them to condemn others and take out their anger and frustration on students.

Acceptance and Unconditional Positive Regard. The facilitating teacher is able to prize the student as a person of worth. The learner's feelings, opinions, and ideas are accepted in an unconditional way. This does not mean that the student's behavior is necessarily condoned. Instead, it means that the teacher cares about the student as a person striving to mature and is able to communicate this sense of caring.

Empathic Understanding. This type of understanding occurs when the teacher can see how things seem to students and communicate an understanding of students' perceptions, opinions and feelings. Rogers contends that teachers seldom communicate empathic understanding. He believes that if teachers would use only a few empathic responses with students each day, this could have a constructive effect on the student-teacher relationship. Much more will be said about these kinds of responses later in this chapter.

Summarizing

In summary, the student-centered classroom is based upon the following principles:

1. Students are perceived as basically good, cooperative and constructive. They will cooperate as partners in the learning process. They are naturally curious and want to learn about things which are relevant to their lives.

2. Students learn best when they perceive subject matter as having relevance for their lives.

3. Frequently, meaningful learning involves experiencing with practical and real problems. Relevance is automatically built into this kind of learning situation.

4. Students need to participate in the learning experience by setting their own objectives, planning how to meet these objectives, and

carrying out their plan. This type of self-initiated learning is inherently relevant.

5. Learning involves the whole person. This includes feelings, attitudes, and beliefs as well as intellect. It is only when the whole person is involved that learning is incorporated into one's self-structure.

6. The learning environment should encourage independence, exploration, creativity, and self-reliance. This environment should be free from threat, criticism and ridicule from outside sources.

7. Self-evaluation of one's accomplishments should be primary while evaluation by others should be secondary.

8. The teacher should be a facilitator of learning rather than an authority who imparts knowledge.

9. To facilitate learning the teacher must establish a relationship with students which is characterized by genuineness, unconditional positive regard, and empathic understanding.

Practical Usefulness. An educational system based on Rogers' approach would require many changes by teachers, administrators, school boards and parents. Such a restructuring of the educational system may be impossible. What, then, can the individual teacher learn from the humanistic orientation which can be useful in managing students' behavior? Thomas Gordon's teacher effectiveness training approach provides an answer to this question. We will now direct our attention to this practical approach with the purpose of exploring how humanistic ideas can be used in a more traditional classroom setting.

Teacher Effectiveness Training

Just as client-centered therapy stresses the relationship between therapist and client, teacher effectiveness training stresses the importance of the relationship between teacher and student. According to Gordon (1974), the crucial factor important to effective teaching is the teacher's ability to establish a special kind of relationship with students. Therefore, teacher effectiveness training focuses on how teachers can establish and maintain effective student-teacher relationships.

The Matter of Problem Ownership

There are many different kinds of problem behaviors which occur in the classroom. It is helpful to think of these behaviors in terms of problem ownership. Frequently teachers are confronted with two types of student behaviors which place special demands on the teacher's ability to manage the classroom effectively. These are behaviors which involve student owned problems and behaviors which involve teacher owned problems.

When the student experiences a problem which does not affect the teacher's ability to manage the classroom situation, the student owns the problem. It is likely that the following examples fall in this category:

* Johnny is upset because he has been cut from the basketball team.

* Lynn, a second grader, is crying because one of her friends has criticized her art work.

* Dick is irritated because he has failed a math quiz.

* Leigh cannot decide whether to take typing or home economics.

In many instances students communicate these kinds of problems to their teacher. A student may express disappointment over not making the team or frustration over doing poorly on a test. The student's comments may indicate concern about the problem but the behavior of the student does not interfere with the teacher's effectiveness in managing the classroom. The student clearly owns the problem. In these instances Gordon believes the teacher has a special role to play in helping students cope with their problems.

Student Owned Problems
and Active Listening

No doubt at some time in the past you have listened to a student or friend discuss a problem. Perhaps you realize how easy it is to discount their problem or even suggest your own solution to their dilemma. If

103

you recall, however, the humanistic viewpoint perceives individuals as basically capable and therefore possessing the ability to resolve their own problems if given the proper help. This viewpoint is reflected in Gordon's advice to teachers concerning how to handle situations when the student owns the problem. Teachers can help students solve problems by using what is referred to as active listening. This type of listening involves both acceptance and understanding and is similar to Rogers' unconditional positive regard and empathic understanding. When a student makes a statement the teacher accepts both the words and the underlying feeling being expressed and communicates this understanding to the student in the form of a feedback message. Here is an example of the use of active listening.

Student: Do we have to write that term paper you told us about?

Teacher: Sounds like you're really worried about that term paper assignment. (Here the teacher guesses that the underlying feeling being expressed by the student is worry. The teacher, therefore, feeds back to the student what the teacher perceives to be an accurate reflection of the student's feeling.)

Student: Well, yes, but not just writing the paper, it's those footnotes I never can get right. (The teacher's previous response has accurately identified the feeling but the student then goes on to clarify specifically what is worrying him.)

Teacher: You've always had trouble with the footnote part.

Student: Yeah, I think I need special help on that.

In this conversation the teacher sensed accurately the underlying feeling although the exact reason for the worry was not pinpointed in the first teacher statement. However, since the general nature of the teacher's statement was on target with what the student was feeling and saying, it was easy for the student to continue by clarifying exactly what was bothering him. It was possible, then, for the teacher to be more specific in his second response. Here are some other examples of active listening in situations where students own the problem.

104

Student: Everybody is always telling you what to do around this school. Why don't they let us do what we want to do sometimes?

Teacher: Sounds like you'd be happier if you got to make some decisions around here occasionally.

. . . . .

Student: I'm not going to gym class today. I can't stand that class anyway!

Teacher: Something about gym class really turns you off.

. . . . .

Student: Nobody around here likes me. I wish I could go to another school.

Teacher: You feel pretty lonely around this place.

Gordon (1974) believes that to be able to use active listening teachers must have a special attitude concerning students and their problems. This attitude includes the following:

1. Teachers must believe that students are capable of resolving and working through their problems even when the process of finding a solution takes time.

2. Teachers must be willing to accept students' feelings in a non-judgmental way regardless of how different these feelings are from what the teacher thinks is appropriate.

3. Teachers must have a desire to help students defuse or release feelings and understand that feelings are often quite transitory.

4. The teacher must be willing to allow time for active listening (pp. 75-76).

According to Gordon (1974), teachers who use active listening find that it "helps students deal with and defuse strong feelings, facilitates problem solving by the student, keeps the responsibility with the student for analyzing his problems, makes students more willing to listen to teachers, and promotes a closer, more meaningful relationship between a teacher and a student" (pp. 78-79).

105

If active listening can be so effective, why do people not use it more frequently? Probably because individuals are not taught to respond in this way. It is more natural to respond by taking your own frame of reference when listening to someone's problem. This leads to various responses such as making suggestions, offering solutions, judging, analyzing and probing. If these kinds of responses are offered when a student owns the problem, the teacher is not allowing the student an opportunity to grapple with the problem, to deal with feelings or to find his own personal solution to the dilemma. As Yelon and Weinstein (1977) point out, "to the extent that they [students] learn to rely on their own resources, trust their own feelings and live with the consequences of their own decisions, they will develop self-confidence, autonomy, and independence" (p. 406).

Levels of Listening

Since active listening is so crucial to helping students deal with their problems, different levels of listening have been analyzed. The levels mentioned below are based upon Carkhuff's Empathy Scale* (Carkhuff, 1969), and indicate how some responses communicate very little understanding while others communicate a high degree of understanding. In the following discussion five levels of listening will be identified and examples of each listening level will be given.

At the <u>first</u> <u>level</u> the responses of the teacher do not attend to the statements of the student. That is, the teacher focuses on things extraneous to the student's statements. This level is characterized by advice giving, lecturing or questioning without considering the student's expressions. In addition, the student's expressed feelings are ignored.

Student: I don't see how learning history is going to help me in any way.

Teacher: Be quiet. I've had enough out of you for one day.

---

*These listening levels are modified from Carkhuff's Empathy Scale. Although these are not presented by Gordon, they will help illustrate the difference between high and low levels of active listening and empathic understanding.

At **level** <u>two</u>, the teacher is attentive to the content of the student's statements. Discussion is limited to the content of what has been expressed and the feelings of the student are ignored. Explanations and questions are characteristic of level two responses.

Student: I don't see how learning history is going to help me in any way.

Teacher: It is going to help you because some day you are going to need it when you go to college.

At **level** <u>three</u>, the teacher perceives and communicates the expressed feeling and meaning of the student's statements. At this level, the teacher is trying to see things exactly as the student has expressed them and to communicate this understanding. The teacher is able to restate in his own words what the student has said. Restatements are, therefore, characteristic of this level.

Student: I don't see how learning history is going to help me in any way.

Teacher: You don't feel that history has any relevance to you.

At **level** <u>four</u>, the teacher not only perceives the expressed feelings of the student but also is able to go beyond what the student has expressed to communicate the student's underlying feelings. A teacher response at this level involves more than simply a restatement of the student's expressed feelings. This response is more of an accurate inference of a feeling which the student has not directly expressed or of which the student is not immediately aware.

Student: I don't see how learning history is going to help me in any way.

Teacher: History doesn't seem to have any relevance to you, therefore it is a bit frustrating to have to spend time on it.

At the <u>fifth</u> **level**, the teacher perceives and communicates the underlying feeling of the student so well that he can explore with the student the important aspects of his present situation.

Student: I don't see how learning history is going to help me in any way.

Teacher: Since history concerns only the past, you
           don't see any relationship between it and
           your life. It's frustrating to have to spend
           time on it. You'd really rather be doing
           something else right now that makes more
           sense to you.

The higher level responses characterize active
listening. Therefore, a response characteristic of
level three, four, or five communicates more understanding of how a person feels than a level one or two
response.

Teacher Owned Problems and
Ineffective Ways of Responding

If you recall, it was mentioned that there are two
types of student behaviors which place special demands
on the teacher--behaviors which involve student-owned
problems and behaviors which involve teacher-owned
problems. At times the behavior of a student will
directly affect the teacher's ability to manage the
classroom or will interfere in some way with the teacher's ability to satisfy a need. When this occurs
Gordon states that the teacher owns the problem. It
is classified in this way because the student's behavior does not present a problem for the student since
his needs are being met. Instead, the teacher is faced
with a problem which is brought about by the student's
behavior.

The following examples are likely to involve
teacher-owned problems:

* Carl constantly interrupts the teacher while she
  is talking.

* Jane and Cathy pass notes to each other during
  math class.

* Todd throws a paper airplane across the room.

* Mary copies her homework from one of her friends.

Gordon believes there are clues which may help
teachers identify teacher-owned problem situations.
These clues come from the teacher's feelings and the
physical reactions to these feelings. When teachers
feel annoyed, angry, frustrated, tense, or upset they
must own these feelings and accept responsibility for
the problem associated with these responses.

When the teacher owns the problem there are three possible ways of responding. The teacher may attempt to (1) modify his own definition or perception of the situation so that the behavior is no longer perceived as a problem, (2) modify the environment so that it is unlikely that the behavior will reoccur, or (3) modify the behavior of the student.

Although the first two approaches may be possible at times, usually the teacher is interested in the latter approach. It is this approach--the attempt to modify the student's behavior--which receives the bulk of the attention in teacher effectiveness training.

Of all the problems which teachers face, none is more critical to effective classroom management than the problem confronted by the teacher when attempting to change student behavior. Gordon believes that teachers frequently use ineffective methods when dealing with teacher-owned problem situations. These ineffective ways of controlling students' behavior include the teacher's use of solution messages and put-down messages. A solution message tells the student what he should do to solve the teacher's problem while a put-down message attacks the self-worth of the student through the use of criticism, ridicule or sarcasm. Here are some examples of solution and put-down messages:

* Get back to work this minute or you'll stay in at recess.

* One more word out of you and you'll go to the principal's office.

* You people are terrible. I leave you for just one minute and look what happens.

* I've never seen anyone as uncooperative as you.

* Go work by yourself. You can't work with the group without disturbing others.

Although the use of "solution" and "put-down" messages is quick and easy to apply, Gordon believes that neither is effective since both elicit negative responses from students such as resistance, rebellion, and anger. When these messages are used students make negative inferences about a teacher, e.g., "he's unfair" or "she's narrow-minded." Since "solution" and "put-down" messages have these undesirable consequences teachers should look for other approaches when attempting to modify student behavior.

An Alternative Response: The I-Message

When a teacher communicates by sending a "solution" or "put-down" message, the teacher communicates information about the student or the student's behavior. This information is contained in a "you" statement where "you" is either clearly stated or implied. When teachers analyze their communication with students, they frequently find that in confronting students most of their messages are "you" messages.

According to Gordon, an I-message is a more appropriate response for the teacher to make when the teacher owns the problem. These messages usually contain the pronoun "I" and communicate how the teacher feels about the behavior which is creating a problem for the teacher. There are three parts to an effective I-message. First, there is a statement identifying the behavior which is creating a problem. This should be a factual statement and must exclude any attempt by the teacher to evaluate the student because of his actions. Second, the concrete effect of the student's behavior on the teacher should be defined. This is important becuase the student will be more motivated to change if he understands how his behavior causes a problem for the teacher. Third, the I-message should include a statement indicating how the student's behavior makes the teacher feel, e.g., upset, frustrated, fearful, angry. Several examples will illustrate the I-message.

* When you interrupt me when I'm talking (behavior) I get upset (feeling) because I have to repeat the instructions (concrete effect).

* I really feel frustrated (feeling) when you don't even try to do your homework (behavior) because then I have to give you a poor grade (concrete effect).

* When you push like that in the lunch line (behavior) it worries me (feeling) since you might get hurt and I'd have to take you to the nurse (concrete effect).

You may wonder why the teacher should go to the trouble of sending an I-message. There are several reasons. I-messages are honest messages which

communicate to the student in a straightforward manner
what is bothering the teacher. These messages allow
the teacher to own her own feelings rather than to
repress them. At the same time the I-message leaves
the responsibility for behavior change with the student. Remember, the humanist believes that given the
opportunity the individual can be responsible and
cooperative. And also important, the I-message does
not contain a negative evaluation of the student as a
you-message frequently does. Therefore, when sending
an I-message the relationship between student and
teacher is not harmed and can even be enhanced since
the teacher has been honest in expressing his feelings
and has shown an ability to trust the student to help
solve the problem.

If students accept the responsibility imposed by
the I-message they will modify their behavior and the
teacher's problem may be solved. In other instances
the teacher's I-message may cause problems for the
student, especially if the student believes that he is
unable to change his behavior due to outside factors.
Take for example the student who comes late for class.

Teacher: I really get irritated when you come late for
a test since I have to repeat the instructions over again.

The teacher's I-message may present a problem for
the student who responds by telling the teacher about
his problem. In situations of this kind it is important for the teacher to be able to switch back to an
active listening response. The dialogue might go like
this.

Student: I can't help being late when Mr. Smith won't
let us out of gym class on time.

Teacher: You think he had something to do with it.

Student: I know he did. From now on I'm going to
have to remind him of the time.

In teacher effectiveness training, teachers are
instructed to recognize those situations where they
should switch from I-messages to active listening.

A Comment About Active Listening
and I-Messages

It is very difficult to use active listening or

111

I-messages successfully if the teacher is not convinced that students are capable of solving their own problems and willing to help solve the teacher's problems. There are teachers who do not have this positive attitude toward students. For these teachers to attempt to fake such an attitude by using active listening and I-messages would be untrue to themselves. When considering the different attitudes of teachers and the behavior of students, it is interesting to wonder whether the self-fulfilling prophecy is involved. To what extent do teachers who view students as capable and cooperative reflect this attitude in their actions and find that their expectations come to pass in the behavior of their students? On the other hand, to what extent do teachers who view students as incapable and uncooperative reflect this attitude in their actions and find that students behave accordingly?

When I-Messages Fail

Gordon concedes that there will be times when I-messages are not effective and the student continues to behave in ways which interfere with the needs of the teacher. Conflict is a fact of life. It usually occurs in every situation in which there is close and continuing contact between individuals. Certainly the student-teacher relationship is no exception.

When there is a strong conflict of needs between student and teacher, I-messages may not be effective simply because the students' needs are so strong that they are not motivated to change or possibly because the student-teacher relationship has deteriorated to such a low level that the students no longer care. In situations where this occurs, Gordon concludes that the needs of both student and teacher are involved in the conflict and that both parties own the problem. The important question then becomes: How do the teacher and student go about resolving the conflict?

Typical Methods Used to Resolve Conflict

Usually teachers use one of two methods in attempting to resolve conflict. Either they use an authoritarian approach (Method I) in which the teacher wins and the student loses or a permissive approach (Method II) in which the student wins and the teacher loses. Both of these methods have serious limitations. If a teacher uses power in a way which is perceived by the student as unfair, this is destructive to the student-teacher relationship. Even though the use of power derived from the teacher's ability to reward and punish may work to control students, the serious limitations associated with its use may outweigh the advantages. Gordon lists a number of dangers inherent in the teacher's use of power. The following two limitations reflect his position.

1. The teacher will eventually run out of power. Younger children are more dependent on the teacher and therefore can be controlled more easily by the teacher's use of power. Older students, especially adolescents, are less dependent on the teacher and less likely to be motivated by the rewards and punishments the teacher can utilize.

2. The teacher's use of power is destructive to students. This can be seen in the behavior students learn as they try to adjust. Such reactions as rebelling, retaliating, lying, cheating, dropping out, and passively submitting are all mentioned by Gordon as possible responses to power.

On the other hand, if the teacher gives in to the power of the student (Method II), the teacher may develop negative attitudes toward students and seek to compensate for losing. These teachers may attempt to get back at students by using subtle methods which put the student in his place, such as giving pop tests or grading examinations harshly. If students continue to win in what is viewed as a power struggle, then the teacher may completely lose the ability to manage the classroom environment.

Conflict Resolution:
The No-Lose Approach

Since there are so many negative consequences to using power to resolve conflict, Gordon suggests an alternative (Method III), which is referred to as the no-lose method. This method does not view the conflict situation as one in which someone must win and someone must lose. Instead, if this approach is used, the student and teacher work together to find a mutually acceptable solution to the problem. This approach to problem resolution has been utilized in certain settings, e.g., industry, for many years. Although educational institutions have frequently ignored a no-lose approach, Gordon believes it can be highly effective in dealing with conflict between teacher and student.

The No-Lose Method: How It Works

To utilize the no-lose method, the teacher must understand the process involved in mutual problem solving. This process takes time to implement and requires a belief on the part of the teacher that students will cooperate to make things better. Gordon believes that if this approach is to be successful the teacher must communicate the following attitude.

"I refuse to use my power at the expense of your losing but I also refuse to let you win at the expense of my losing. I want to respect your needs but I also must respect my own. Let's find a new approach that will help us find a solution that will meet both your needs and mine. The solution we're after is one that will allow us both to win" (1974, p. 227).

The communication of this attitude provides the necessary groundwork for the implementation of the problem-solving process. This process involves the following six steps:

1. Defining the problem.

2. Generating possible solutions.

3. Evaluating the solution.

4. Deciding which solution is best.

5. Determining how to implement the decision.

6. Assessing how well the solution solves the problem.

The first step, defining the problem, is of critical importance. Gordon's experience has been that when the no-lose method fails, it is frequently due to a breakdown at step one. At this point it is essential for the teacher to clearly state the problem in terms of unmet needs without suggesting a solution. For example, "I need quiet in the room so that I can give the instructions." The teacher's use of an I-message without telling students how to solve the problem allows students to talk about their own needs and perhaps send an I-message of their own. As students

114

respond it is important for the teacher to use active listening so that students can express their needs and be understood. After defining the problem in this manner, the teacher and students then suggest possible solutions. All suggested solutions should be accepted without judgment or evaluation during step two. After the solutions have been presented, then the teacher and students eliminate any suggestions which are unacceptable. No suggestion should be kept as a possible solution at this stage if it is unacceptable to any party to the conflict. The solutions which have not been eliminated are then discussed to arrive at the one solution which is most agreeable to both students and teacher. No solution should be agreed upon until parties to the conflict indicate a willingness to try a particular solution. The agreed-upon solution is then clearly stated in writing and plans for implementation are discussed. The last step calls for an assessment of the agreed-upon solution after a trial period of time. The no-lose method can be used not only when conflict arises between students and teacher but also when the teacher works with the class to set rules or when two or more students disagree among themselves.

As the teacher and students participate in the no-lose method, a positive ongoing relationship develops which leads to more mature and responsible behavior on the part of students. According to advocates of teacher effectiveness training, this approach to classroom management leads to less resentment toward the teacher, fewer disciplinary problems and a better climate for student learning to take place.

A Comment on Research Support

Humanistic educators frequently provide support for their approach by presenting diaries or case examples of teachers who have been successful utilizing the humanistic approach. This is the case with the advocates of teacher effectiveness training. Gordon presents teacher testimonials as evidence of now teacher effectiveness training has been beneficial to those who have implemented his suggestions. Examples of such testimonials are presented in Gordon's book Teacher Effectiveness Training.

There is also a growing body of research which lends support to the effectiveness of a humanistic approach. Although this research does not specifically test teacher effectiveness training concepts, it does examine certain principles upon which Gordon's approach is based. The following case examples will present three studies characteristic of this research.

CASE EXAMPLE 4-1

Aspy, D. N. "The Effect of Teacher Offered Condi-
tions of Empathy, Positive Regard and Congruence Upon
Student Achievement." Florida Journal of Educational
Research, 1969, 11 (1), 39-48.

Studies indicate that a positive classroom climate
affects student learning. In this study the researcher
investigated the effect of different levels of teacher
empathy, congruence and positive regard on the academic
progress of students. One hundred and twenty third-
graders were matched according to I.Q. and sex. These
students were administered five subtests of the Stan-
ford Achievement Test at the beginning and end of the
academic school year. The six teachers of the subject
group submitted tape recordings of their reading
classes for analysis. Raters, experienced at assessing
the conditions being studied, rated random segments of
the tapes using scales specifically developed for
measuring empathy, positive regard and congruence.

Three teachers were rated high on these conditions
while three were rated low. The difference between the
two groups was found to be significant. Therefore,
students of the teachers rated high received higher
levels of empathy, congruence and positive regard than
students of teachers rated low. The results indicated
that those students receiving high levels of the facilitative conditions made more overall gains on the Stan-
ford Achievement Test. On four of the five subtests
(language, word meaning, word study skills and paragraph meaning) and on the total gain score, the gains
made by the students of high functioning teachers were
significantly greater than the gains made by students
of the low functioning teachers. For the total gain
score the difference between the means for the two
groups was 1.6 years. Only on the spelling subtest was
a non-significant difference found between the two
groups, with students in the lower group receiving
slightly higher gains. High levels of empathy, positive regard, and congruence were associated with high
achievement whereas low levels of these conditions were
associated with low achievement.

Dixon, W. R., and Morse, W. C. "The Prediction of Teacher Performance: Empathic Potential." _Journal_ _of_ _Teacher_ _Education_, 1961, 12, 322-329.

For years educators have been interested in predicting the level of a teacher's performance. Dixon and Morse administered various tests to a group of 97 student teachers. These researchers also assessed the attitudes of over 2,000 high school students taught by these student teachers and evaluated ratings of these teachers made by their supervisors. The researchers were especially interested in (1) determining if students would evaluate "good" empathy teachers as better teachers than "poor" empathy teachers, (2) assessing the evaluations of supervising teachers to see if any differences would exist between the evaluations of "good" and "poor" empathy teachers, (3) determining if teachers rated "good" in empathic ability would evaluate themselves differently than the teachers rated "poor"; and (4) discovering whether teachers who felt more positive toward students would differ in their appraisal of themselves as measured by the Teacher Self-Concept Inventory.

The findings support a relationship between empathic responding and teacher ratings. "Good" empathy teachers were evaluated as better teachers by both students and supervising teachers than were "poor" empathy teachers. Furthermore, teachers who felt very positive toward their students were significantly more stable in their appraisal of themselves as teachers as measured by the Teacher Self-Concept Inventory.

CASE EXAMPLE 4-3

Lewis, A. L., Lovell, J. T., and Jessee, B. E.
"Interpersonal Relationship and Pupil Progress." Personnel and Guidance Journal, 1965, 44, 396-401.

In this study the researchers hypothesized that
students who perceive the relationship with their
teacher as being somewhat like the ideal therapeutic
relationship will make greater academic gains than
students who do not perceive the student-teacher relationship in this way. The subjects of this study con-
sisted of sixth and ninth grade students from a middle
class suburban area. Each student in these grades (644
sixth graders and 845 ninth graders) was given the
Teacher-Pupil Relationship Inventory. This inventory
assesses the student's perception of the relationship
established by the teacher on such characteristics as
understanding, trust, and genuineness. The sixth grade
teachers had the students in class for the entire day,
whereas the ninth grade teachers taught the students
only one subject (English). The teachers administered
standardized tests at both the beginning and end of the
year. The Iowa Test of Basic Skills was used with the
sixth graders and the English Achievement subtests of
the Iowa Test of Educational Development was used with
the ninth graders.

For both grades six and nine a high relationship
score group and a low relationship score group were
established, consisting of eighty-six sixth graders and
seventy-six ninth graders. The findings indicated that
the sixth grade students who rated their teacher high,
i.e., established a therapeutic-like relationship, made
significantly greater gains on the Iowa Test of Basic
Skills over the course of the year than did students
who rated their teacher low. For the ninth graders,
the students of high rated teachers made greater
achievement gains than the students of low rated
teachers but the difference in gains was not found to
be significant. The fact that the sixth grade teachers
had the students throughout the day while the ninth
grade teachers had the students for only one class has
been given as a reason for the difference in findings
between grade levels. Nevertheless, the finding,
especially with sixth graders, lends support to the
importance of the relationship between student and
teacher.

INVOLVEMENT EXERCISES

1. Give some examples of classroom situations where the teacher owns the problem.

2. If possible, compare your above examples with the examples of other teachers and note similarities and differences. Why do differences exist?

3. Boxes number 1 and number 2 below divide students' behavior into two categories, acceptable behavior and unacceptable behavior, for two teachers who teach similar classes. You can see that Ms. Green is able to accept much of her students' behavior while Ms. Jones finds much of her students' behavior unacceptable. In box number 3, draw a line which you believe characterizes yourself in relation to acceptance and unacceptance of your students' behavior.

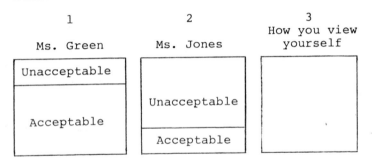

Describe what you believe Ms. Green and Ms. Jones Would be like as teachers.

Describe the person characterized by box number 3.

List some factors which might cause the line between acceptable and unacceptable behavior to move up or down even for the same teacher.

4. Practice using active listening in the following examples where the student owns the problem.

Student
(4th grade):
My daddy said he would beat me if I didn't start doing better in math.

Teacher:

Student
(6th grade):
I hate these standardized tests. They just give them to find out how stupid we are.

Teacher:

Student
(9th grade):
Everybody is always telling us what to do around this place. It's like a jailhouse. Why don't they let us do what we want to do sometimes?

Teacher:

Student
(2nd grade):
I'm sorry I forgot my homework. I did it (starts to cry). I promise I did it last night and just forgot it.

Teacher:

Student
(high school):
I can't get this math stuff. There's not anything I can do—even my parents say that. They don't even care what happens to me.

Teacher:

Student
(3rd grade):
Tommy said my art work wasn't any good. What does he know anyway. He's so dumb.

Teacher:

121

5. In the following situations, the teacher owns the problem. Put yourself in the teacher's place and construct an I-message which includes a description of behavior, the effect of behavior and how you feel.

Situation: Sylvia continues to interrupt the
7th grade   teacher to ask inappropriate ques-
                    tions while the teacher is dis-
                    cussing the day's lesson with the
                    class.

I-Message:

Situation: Tommy, one of your mischievous
5th grade   fourth graders, hides the chalkboard
                    erasers so you cannot find them.

I-Message:

Situation: Pat has gone to the board to work a
6th grade   math problem. When he finishes he
                    writes a dirty word on the board
                    and the students laugh and joke
                    about it.

I-Message:

Situation: Susan throws several pieces of
high school   paper at the trash can in a basket-
                    ball type fashion during a history
                    quiz. Several pieces miss the can
                    and hit another student.

I-Message:

6. When I-messages don't work, Gordon suggests Method III (the no-lose method) to solve conflicts. Indicate how you would go through the six steps of the no-lose method to resolve a conflict in your classroom.

7. Write a paragraph stating your views on the following question: To what extent do you believe that students are innately good and that this goodness must be nurtured in order for them to develop in positive ways?

REFERENCES

Baron, R., Byrne, D., and Kantowitz, B. _Psychology: Understanding behavior_. Philadelphia: W. B. Saunders, 1977.

Carkhuff, R. R. _Helping and human relations_, Vol. II. New York: Holt, Rinehart, and Winston, 1969.

Combs, A. _The professional education of teachers: a humanistic approach to teacher preparation_. Boston: Allyn and Bacon, 1974.

Corey, G. _Theory and practice of counseling and psychotherapy_. Belmont, Col.: Brooks/Cole, 1977.

Gordon, Thomas. _P.E.T.: Parent effectiveness training_. New York: Peter H. Wyden, 1974.

Gordon, Thomas. _T.E.T.: Teacher effectiveness training_. New York: Peter M. Wyden, 1974.

Patterson, C. H. _Foundations for a theory of instruction and educational psychology_. New York: Harper and Row, 1977.

Rogers, C. "A theory of therapy, personality, and interpersonal relationships, as developed in the client-centered framework." In S. Koch (Ed.), _Psychology: A study of a science_ (Vol. 3). New York: McGraw Hill, 1959.

Rogers, C. _Client-centered therapy_. Boston: Houghton Mifflin, 1951.

Rogers, C. _Freedom to learn: A view of what education might become_. Columbus, Ohio: Merrill Publishing Co., 1969.

Rogers, C. _On becoming a person_. Boston: Houghton Mifflin, 1961.

Rogers, C. "The conditions of change from a client-centered viewpoint." In B. Berenson and R. Carkhuff (Eds.), _Sources of gain in counseling and psychotherapy_. New York: Holt, Rinehart and Winston, 1967.

Rogers, C. "Toward a modern approach to values: The valuing process in the mature person." _The

124

Journal of Abnormal and Social Psychology, 1964, 68, 160-167.

Rogers, Carl. Counseling and psychotherapy. Boston: Houghton Mifflin, 1942.

Yelon, S., and Weinstein, G. A teacher's world: Psychology in the classroom. New York: McGraw-Hill, 1977.